BFI Modern Classics

Rob White
Series Editor

Advancing into its second century, the cinema is now a mature art form
with an established list of classics. But contemporary cinema is so
subject to every shift in fashion regarding aesthetics, morals and ideas
that judgments on the true worth of recent films are liable to be risky
and controversial; yet they are essential if we want to know where the
cinema is going and what it can achieve.

As part of the British Film Institute's commitment to the
promotion and evaluation of contemporary cinema, and in conjunction
with the influential BFI Film Classics series, BFI Modern Classics is a
series of books devoted to individual films of recent years. Distinguished
film critics, scholars and novelists explore the production and reception
of their chosen films in the context of an argument about the film's
quality and importance. Insightful, considered, often impassioned, these
elegant, well-illustrated books will set the agenda for debates about what
matters in modern cinema.

Blue Velvet

Michael Atkinson

BFI PUBLISHING

First published in 1997 by the
BRITISH FILM INSTITUTE
21 Stephen St, London W1P 2LN

The British Film Institute exists to promote
appreciation, enjoyment, protection and
development of moving image culture in and
throughout the whole of the United Kingdom.
Its activities include the National Film and
Television Archive; the National Film Theatre;
the Museum of the Moving Image;
the London Film Festival; the production and
distribution of film and video; funding and
support for regional activities; Library and
Information Services; Stills, Posters and
Designs; Research; Publishing and Education;
and the monthly *Sight and Sound* magazine.

Designed by Andrew Barron &
Collis Clements Associates

Typeset in Garamond Simoncini
by Fakenham Photosetting Limited,
Fakenham, Norfolk

Printed in Great Britain

Picture editing by Millie Simpson

British Library Cataloguing-in-Publication Data
A catalogue record for this book is available
from the British Library.
ISBN 0–85170–559–6

Contents

Dedication

For Laurel and Molly

Acknowledgments

My thanks for contributed ideas and assistance with this pint-sized text to Paul D. Sammon, Virginia Campbell, Gavin Smith, Gerald Cuesta, Chris Wales and Frank Gallagher.

Picture credits

BFI Stills, Posters and Designs (cover). All pictures from BFI Stills, Posters and Designs except: Moviestore Collection (pp. 3, 7, 38, 51, 74); Ronald Grant Collection (pp. 2, 15, 30, 39, 47, 55, 59, 75).

Isabella Rosselini as Dorothy Valens

1

Forest, I fear you!
    Baudelaire (trans. Richard Howard)

Taken on any level, David Lynch's *Blue Velvet* is an utterly unique act of cinema: an 80s Hollywood studio film as radical, visionary and cabalistic as anything found in the avant-garde; a mysteriously symbolic and subterranean 'cult' movie that nevertheless has recognisable stars and was broadly distributed; a genre piece with the ambience of a fearsome, hypercomposed nightmare; an American 'art film' by Hollywood's only reputable 'art film' director – a startling anomaly in itself, and if the label seems inappropriate, find another. Art film traditions have had, at any rate, little influence on the film's hermetic topoi. Its roots are in different and widely disparate soils, which we will explore. But more than nearly any movie – even *Eraserhead* – *Blue Velvet* owes its unique flavour and texture to its director's own subconscious will. Its richness as a text and as a filmic experience derives precisely from the disquieting friction between its maker's psychosexual impulses and the workaday realities of movie plot, action and character. Its singular accomplishment rests in the simultaneous control and unleashing of the irrational.

    This may make *Blue Velvet* sound merely 'surrealist' – an aesthetic docket that today taints more than it enlightens. More to the point, Lynch's imagery is far from what is manifestly defined as 'surrealist', which, in its truest, uncommodified form, is pathmarked by a sociological absurdism – that is, it retains power only as it roasts bourgeois desires and mocks social taboos. As a serious artistic strategy, cinematic surrealism per se (outside of various commercial appropriations and the mordantly particular voices of Luis Buñuel and Jan Svankmajer) hasn't survived well into and beyond the post-modern era precisely *because* of its dependence upon social affront and upon the disorientation of dream reasoning in everyday contexts.

    Perhaps cinema as an experience is already too deeply soaked in

subconscious spirits to support wilful irrationality as a principle –
which may be why dreams in films always seem silly and redundant.
(As J. Hoberman pointed out, for Lynch, 'the normal is a defense
against the irrational rather than vice versa'.[1]) An artist of
unquestionable uniqueness, Lynch has always effortlessly been able to
circumnavigate such potholes – his best films don't resemble dreams as
much as a version of reality sick with the poison of dream-making.
As Virginia Campbell wrote in *Movieline*, Lynch proceeds *from* dreams
toward ideas, just as Kafka claimed his writing was derived from his
ability to dream while he was awake. 'I think that's the whole thing,'
Lynch agreed. 'Every film is like a waking dream. All the ideas are like
daydreams.'[2] All the same, while *Blue Velvet*'s most peculiar imagery and
most effective textual tropes may be the raw, unreasonable Lynch-stuff

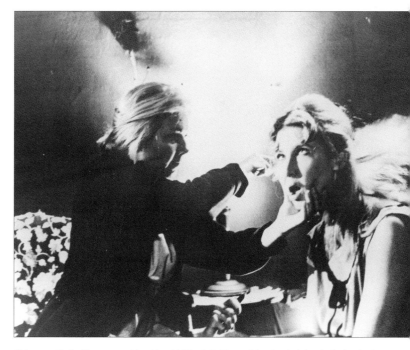

At home with the X's: a convulsing Mary X (Charlotte Stewart) has her hair frantically brushed
out by her mother (Jeanne Bates) in *Eraserhead*

we'd be a fool to celebrate for anything besides its mysteries, the film's framework is overtly, manifestly Freudian, just as are *The Grandmother* (an early Lynch short) and *Eraserhead*. *Blue Velvet*'s oedipal boldness is so overt, in fact, that one never doubts its unconscious source; Lynch was, up to *Blue Velvet* at least, an authentic savage innocent, a cinematic savant whose uninhibited relationship with his own exploding consciousness is unhindered by analysis or traditional principles of order.

The subterranean tension between id and superego is what makes Lynch's imagery so viscerally effective, and is precisely what's lacking in most cinematic strivings toward the surreal. The old lady growing out of a soil-covered mattress in *The Grandmother*; the fishbowl of water and coins hidden in a bureau drawer, the mutant lady in the radiator, and the sequence in which Henry's bed becomes a pond of milk, in *Eraserhead*; the cosmic-cum-industrial aura of *The Elephant Man*'s opening and coda; the use of the severed ear, the beetles and the mechanical robin in *Blue Velvet* – they're all images that tug between pure dream and an undecipherable narrative logic, half Freudian and half bughouse qualm. Lynch is often quoted as saying he chooses his imagery and iconography just because 'it feels right',[3] adopting a fey yet consistent surrender to his own non-linear thinking. Perhaps that is Lynch's most intimidating achievement: the unquestionable triumph of a mode of impulsive artistic syllogisation that for other practitioners is often a straight, fast flight into the brick wall of self-indulgence, cheap pretension and sophomoric shock.

Thus, Lynch can be seen as the preternaturally gifted cousin of an irresponsible, ne'er-do-well image-maker like Alexander Jodorowsky, and it's a telling detail that they were both chosen by Dino de Laurentiis to adapt *Dune*. (In either case, though, Dino's choice was off the beam.) Lynch's vision often seems genuinely a priori, and though *Blue Velvet* could be characterised as a fetishistic neo-noir or an absurdist Hardy Boys mystery or a Sade-inflected *Bildungsfilm* or an interrogation of post-war Middle America, as well as a lurid oedipal struggle, it most often seems to have crawled fully formed from Lynch's damp and ill-lit brainpan. Indeed, isn't the rare film capable of fulfilling so many diagnoses best served by allowing them all to stand? Lynch, we can presume, would shrug off all such discussion – it's just his movie, made the way he felt was 'right'.

Blue Velvet is one of the very few seminal films whose seminality was apparent on its very first contact with viewers. There was no question in 1986, in any corner, about its eminence, just as there's been little argument since, despite *Raging Bull* being voted best American film of the 80s by critics, that it's the most influential and crucial film of its decade.[4] For a large percentage of critics as well as audiences, it was as if they had never realised the expressive potentialities of film before; for many others, the movie's sui generis rhythms and perverse action comprised a violation of the trust between movie and audience that most film-makers strive to maintain and most filmgoers rely on. (I saw

Rose in bloom:
Dorothy accepting
guests

the film on opening night in a crowded suburban Long Island theatre, where the unsuspecting middle-class audience, apparently lured by laudatory reviews, practically rioted – uncomfortable laughter and disoriented conversation quickly gave way to angry shouting, hurled objects at the screen and more walk-outs than I'd ever seen before or since.) It simply did not resemble any movie anyone had ever seen before. Stunned and glowing like the receivers of a holy vision, the critics gushed, eager to articulate what may well have been an inarticulatable experience. J. Hoberman, in *The Village Voice*, frothed, 'There hasn't been an American studio film so rich, so formally controlled, so imaginatively cast and wonderfully acted, and so charged with its maker's psychosexual energy since *Raging Bull*.'[5] In her dazed, bubbling review, *The New Yorker*'s grande dame Pauline Kael wrote, 'This is American darkness – darkness in color, darkness with a happy ending. Lynch might turn out to be the first populist surrealist – a Frank Capra of dream logic.'[6]

Some critics, however, were as repulsed and befuddled as the opening-day Long Island audience I witnessed. Roger Ebert wrote: 'The movie is pulled so violently in opposite directions that it pulls itself apart.'[7] TV critics in general were roundly appalled; on PBS's *Sneak Previews*, Michael Medved proclaimed it 'plotless, pretentious and putrid', while Rex Reed of *At the Movies* labelled it 'the sickest wallow in filth and sleaze'.[8] (For some reason, Denver, Colorado was particularly hostile – Lynch reportedly even called a disgruntled Denver critic to explain the film to him, and a feature story resulted.[9]) Noir expert/novelist Barry Gifford (whose novel *Wild at Heart* would be adapted by Lynch four years later) blanched in his *Mystery Scene* magazine column, calling the film 'phlegm *noir*', 'one cut above a snuff film', and referring to Lynch as a 'pornographic fabulist'.[10] It'd be fascinating to read Gifford's take now, after seeing what Lynch did to his novel – which is to say, thoroughly Lynch-ified it – and after that film won top prize at Cannes.

More than most, *Blue Velvet* is a 'personal' film, and even the most dubious auteur-theory agnostic would be compelled to acknowledge its intimate relationship with its writer/director, and the fact that it could never have been made by anyone else. Though Lynch has given many interviews, and spoken somewhat frankly about his childhood and personal life, there remain, not surprisingly, a great many unanswered questions. He is a notoriously ambiguous figure, and the fey, mildly eccentric details about his prim dress style, odd living habits and the unembarrassed, aw-shucks delivery of the most outrageously deranged notions have made great hay for the press at least up to the *Twin Peaks* phenomena. There has never been a Hollywood figure even remotely like him. (I especially like this quote, dished out deadpan to a *Premiere* interviewer, about going to Bob's Big Boy for lunch every day: 'I can think there and draw on the napkins and have my shake. Sometimes I have a cup of coffee and sometimes I have a small Coke. They both go great with shakes. ... I like diners. I don't like dark places.'[11]) Use the films as a lens through which to view what little we know of his life – talking about his younger sister Margaret, for instance (he also has a younger brother, John), he would sometimes say that as a child she 'was afraid of green peas because they were hard on the outside and soft on the inside' and leave it at that[12] – and we come away with perhaps the most unselfconscious, unironic, genuine merging of man and medium the movies have yet seen. There is undoubtedly much we don't understand; Lynch's elusive manner of taletelling may simply be a result, according to Paul D. Sammon, author and ex-studio exec who worked on *Blue Velvet*, of an aesthetic superstition: 'I think he thought that if you speak directly about something, it loses its power.'[13] In any case, as if *Eraserhead* and *Blue Velvet* themselves weren't sufficient indication, Lynch is not like you or me in significant ways, and because there's *so much* of him in *Blue Velvet* the film can scald you with its feverish sensation of ultramundaneness. *Because* of its personalism, it can feel like observing brain surgery, where the patient is awake and giggling and the tissue itself, as it's probed and explored and cut, remains a disturbing, impenetrable mystery.

A native of Missoula, Montana, born 20 January 1946, Lynch is the eldest of three children, son of a Brooklyn-born housewife and teacher, and a Montana-born research scientist for the Department of Agriculture. His father was a career woodsman ('Like I always say: if you cut my father's leash, he would go into the woods and never come back.'[14]), and his job moved the Lynches from one national forest to another, from Spokane to Arlington. Details (many of them typically, abstrusely Lynchian) could be gathered from Lynch's interviews, but a coherent portrait of his early life would be impossible to muster. Suffice it to say that Lynch's divulged memories of childhood in the north-west have been impressionistic and familiarly unsifted for irony: 'It was a dream world, with a blue sky, planes droning overhead, fences, green grass, cherry trees. … But, on the cherry tree, there's this pitch oozing out – some black, some yellow.'[15] In these honest remarks, Lynch scans like a Peter Pan, never quite growing up into a state of reflective adulthood. 'Rubber toys floated on water,' he explained to the film journal *Positif*. 'Meals seemed to last five hours and naptime seemed endless.'[16]

Suddenly, the turgid heavenliness of the Radiator Lady's song in *Eraserhead*, and the robins-of-love dream recounted by Sandy in *Blue Velvet,* don't seem so odd, or as purely contrapuntal, within their contexts. Lynch's formative, beatific experience of north-western small-town life, and his subsequent disillusionment with adulthood, are obviously the well from which *Blue Velvet* sprang, and, relatedly, *Blue Velvet* is obviously the psychodramatic therapy Lynch had to endure in order to exorcise its demons and lost loves.

The adult path to *Blue Velvet* is by now a famous one: art school (painting was Lynch's first ambition; a book of his paintings and film stills, *Images*, was published by Hyperion in 1994), conceptual student films (animations, perpetual loops, sculptured screens), American Film Institute patronage, the midnight cult success of *Eraserhead*, the fame and esteem of *The Elephant Man*, the gargantuan disaster of *Dune*. According to Sammon, who was then the De Laurentiis Entertainment

Group vice-president of special promotions, Lynch, apparently crushed, took a year off after that debacle and went into seclusion. When he emerged with the script for *Blue Velvet*, Dino greenlighted the project on the condition that Lynch shoot it cheaply at the DEG Studios in Wilmington, North Carolina, and eat most of his own fees. After *Dune*, you'd think De Laurentiis might be queasy about working with Lynch again; more than one critic has referred to his role as *Blue Velvet*'s bankroller as one of money-blind artistic patronage. Hardly so: 'Dino appreciated David's rather bizarre gifts,' Sammon says, 'and besides, Dino's system was to *always* presell everything through his European and international contacts, so he never lost money.'

In various drafts, the screenplay for the film had actually been passed around since the late 70s; as early as the spring of 1981, more

than a year before production had begun on *Dune*, producer Richard Roth announced *Blue Velvet* as one of his upcoming projects.[17] The production was finally announced in August 1984, and the relatively

Frank Booth and his cronies: J. Michael Hunter, Dennis Hopper, Jack Nance, Brad Dourif uneventful (compared to *Dune*, at least) twelve-week shoot began in Wilmington in January 1985.[18]

Throughout Lynch's ascension to fame as a cult auteur (it could be said that Lynch has mainstreamed, and therefore obliterated, what's commonly thought of as 'cult'; ten years after *Blue Velvet* and seven after *Twin Peaks*, the word has little genuine cachet), the man himself showed no signs of industry blight or media 'corruption' – only after the failure of *Fire Walk with Me* and of his three post-*Twin Peaks* TV series did Lynch recede from view. (As of this writing, Lynch is putting the finishing touches on *Lost Highway*, co-written with Gifford.) What's not so popularly known is how close *Blue Velvet* came to being a cultural footnote. According to Sammon, the DEG marketing department were at an utter loss as to how to sell Lynch's hermetic little feverdream. 'No one wanted to touch it with a ten-foot barge pole,' Sammon says. 'The film was looked at as a freak, and I don't think David ever knew.' Sammon, apparently, was the only voice in the whole company who saw the film for the remarkable, quasi-art film entity it was, and he decided to take it on.

Rather than bury it – the consensus among the other executives – Sammon spent more than six months 'platforming' it small, building word-of-mouth by travelling to dozens of film festivals and conventions with a print of the film under his arm. The movie's reputation began to snowball, and DEG as a whole finally took notice, opening the film wide and promoting it full steam. Since, as Sammon puts it, 'marketing departments have an obscene amount of power', it's quite conceivable that had the film not accumulated the devotion of its studio (how many other great movies disappeared for lack of same?), the audience for Lynch's film might have been as peripheral and specialised as the one for *Eraserhead* — the word 'cult' might still apply. Imagine: it might have been snuck out on video or shown only at midnight in suburban theatres, and a small tribe of semi-stoned, alternative movieheads might have been its only ardent supporters.

2

JOHN: Get in the skiff, Pearl, goodness, goodness, *hurry*!
PEARL: (hesitant) That's *Daddy!*
The Night of the Hunter, original screenplay by James Agee

The opening 'overture' of *Blue Velvet* – its magisterial first four minutes, from the sealike, vaguely nauseating undulations of the cobalt velvet curtain under the credits to the subterranean grub's-eye-view close-up of grappling beetles – immediately prepares viewers for the dislocations to come, though the dreamlike montage syntax of this sequence is one Lynch only returns to for the film's coda. Designed to obliterate our perceived notions of cinematic narrative set-up, Lynch's purely imagined

John (Billy Chapin) and Pearl (Sally June Bruce) escape stepfiend Robert Mitchum and begin their dreamy river journey in *The Night of the Hunter*

opening engages a more poetic, elliptical sense of 'cinema', a type of imagistic shorthand that interfaces with Pudovkin, Buñuel and Welles, *The Night of the Hunter*, *Persona* and *The Colour of Pomegranates*. (Hardly radical from the broadest of film history perspectives, Lynch's queer, stilted images are acts of anarchy in the context in which they arose: 80s Hollywood film-making.) Even so, *Blue Velvet* is remarkably unsullied by reflexive or homaging movie knowledge – it's pure. (Explicit references to *The Wizard of Oz*, beyond Dorothy's name, were cut – strains of 'Over the Rainbow', ruby slippers, etc. – and saved for *Wild at Heart*.)

As we see most clearly later in the sequence in which Jeffrey finds the two corpses in Dorothy Vallens's apartment, nobody outside of Sergei Paradjanov has dealt so arrestingly with tableaux vivants in film. (*Eraserhead* stands as exhibit B in this regard.) It's a style that prioritises image resonance over narrative thrust, compositional chill over reason. In *Blue Velvet*'s infamous opening, Lynch dissolves from his creepily tactile credits (and Angelo Badalamenti's hyper-lush introductory theme) to overcomposed, colour-saturated, culturally archetypal Norman Rockwell images set to a dull Muzak version of the titular song: fire-engine-red roses and fluorescent yellow tulips growing against a proverbial white picket fence, an actual fire engine complete with

Entering
Lumberton

smiling firefighter and dalmatian, a crossing guard assuring the safe street-crossing of schoolkids, and, eventually, a well-fed homeowner watering the lawn of his classically tended (though small and, implicitly, lower-middle-class) suburban home.

In these first minutes, cinematographer Frederick Elmes achieved a startlingly fresh, hyperreal look that makes you feel you've never seen a film in colour before. We glimpse the housewife drinking coffee and watching a mysterious TV programme inside (one of Lynch's many gratifying details: an anonymous, decontextualised, noirish shot of a hand holding a gun – *not* in colour – which makes clear how fragmented our vision of the film's mystery will be), before the lurking tensions below this cartoonish portrait of domestic serenity begin to appear: a kink in the garden hose, sputtering with water, frustrates our homeowner until he is abruptly seized by what could either be an internal trauma like a stroke or an aneurysm, or, given the ambiguous grasp at the back of his neck, an insect bite of some unspecified sort. He falls to the grass squirming silently, spurting hose in hand. A yapping dog appears, fiercely lapping at the careening water, and a baby toddles nearby the paralysed figure. Lynch even punctuates this bizarre confluence of images with a slow-motion close-up of the dog biting at

Jeffrey's father (Jack Harvey) succumbs to his indefinable seizure

the arcing stream, as if for a moment to lyricise what has not yet even coalesced, and in many ways never coalesces, into a traditional story. Our shivers are substantiated as Lynch's camera grovels low to the ground, panning and launching into the grass, where, in the soily shadows, the black beetles rumble in uncomfortable close-up. Lynch and 'sound designer' Alan Splet, in the first of the film's many aural masterstrokes, score this sequence with a cacophony of machine noises and bassy mayhem, lending the insects awesome scale and menace. We only see them for a few seconds (Lynch cuts abruptly to a 'Welcome to Lumberton' billboard), but the bugs stay with us – they're portents of horrors we're awaiting from that moment on.

So, immediately the primary layers of the film are articulated – the dark, unstoppable natural forces at work under the careful veneer of small-town America. Which is to say, basically, that the film is a drama of id–ego conflict, even in its soundtrack, colour schemes and incidental design. It's a peeled egg in which the yolk is rotten. While its thematic framework hearkens back to Poe, James and gothic fiction, *Night Must Fall*, *Shadow of a Doubt*, *The Night of the Hunter*, *The Naked Kiss*, and, to a lesser extent, the entire notion of noir (not to mention the crazed suburbia of early John Waters films), *Blue Velvet*'s forthright conception of evil hidden in the mundane, its appalling, inexplicable details and consequences, is so totally original it feels like a film without precedent, without history. And the perverse, almost primitive confidence of the opening sequence proves Lynch knew it – insofar as he had any conscious, or admittable, knowledge at all of his work's affective torque.

Critics knew a fresh vision when they saw it, and the vast majority of commentators held the first four minutes up as what was symptomatic of the film's uniqueness. In fact, the overture has the surface simplicity of fable; the rest of the film hints at mysteries and human depths so purple, fusty and twisted that they lend the naive opening images an extra layer of irony. It's like comparing a single, disturbing dream to the subconscious avalanche of a submerged psychotic. But its vocabulary was simple, and simply startling, so it made for convenient access.

What's most remarkable about the opening montage a decade later is its childlike sweetness, a strange texture that runs throughout Lynch's work, and which here is as purposefully innocent a key to the work as 'Rosebud' was to the life of Charles Foster Kane. It's inadequate textually if we take it as a literal 'introduction', a miniature; it's resoundingly meaningful as an expression of innocent fear and desire, and the subsequent film itself as the trial of maturation.

Which perfectly fits its otherwise overt oedipal schema. Indeed, every frame of the film pulsates with appalled innocence, with the shock of a child trying to come to grips with the adult cosmos. By extension, it's a supreme vision of parental anxiety as well, which is a font of signs and meanings that might easily spawn a genre of film theory all its own in the post-Baby Boomer era to accompany feminist and multicultural schools. (Lynch had two children by the time of *Blue Velvet*.) We first glimpse the film's protagonist, Jeffrey Beaumont (Kyle MacLachlan), walking resignedly through a seedy field of his home town Lumberton, Washington, while on the soundtrack a radio announcer declares 'It's a sunny, woodsy day in Lumberton, so get those chainsaws out . . .': Lynch's childhood familiarity with the northern American forests and their ageing logging towns is evident in his wry and economical portrait of Lumberton, which is, even at first blush, half Andy Hardy homestead, half exhausted industrial ghost town; for every picture-perfect suburban cliché, there are miles of dated, bankrupt riverfront, dead factories and industrial effluvia. 'At the sound of the falling tree,' the announcer continues, followed by the sound of a chainsaw and a tree crashing to the ground, 'it's 9:30! There's a lot of wood waiting out there, so let's get going!' The soundtrack then segues, slyly, to Badalamenti's vampy, vaguely threatening jazz – hardly music the average Lumbertonian would tune in to.

The wood-town interface with Lynch's biography was always taken as read, as was Kyle MacLachlan's resemblance to Lynch and his role as Lynch's screen alter ego. But who has seriously considered *Blue Velvet* as autobiographical, even in a spiritual or psychological sense? Lynch is so deliberately immune to readings of his films, and so withholding of information about himself and his life, that it's a question that may never be satisfactorily answered. Remember, though, that *Blue Velvet* was only his second original feature script (after *Eraserhead*), and one he apparently nursed for years and through several versions, ever since completing *The Elephant Man*. 'I started to get ideas for it in 1973,' he told *Cineaste* in 1987, 'but it was all very vague. I only had a feeling and a title.'[19] *Blue Velvet* is so fertile a text for so many reasons that one can't be blamed for conjecturing on how much of it literally intersects with Lynch's life. The father? The girlfriend? The bully football player named Mike (recurring in *Twin Peaks*)? Dorothy?

Lynch found MacLachlan for *Dune*, and doubtlessly had hopes he could use him in *Blue Velvet*'s particularly self-reflective manner

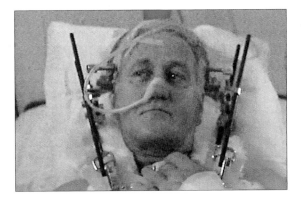

Mr Beaumont in the hospital

sometime after that lumbering, ill-planned sf fiasco had receded into the past. By using MacLachlan as his doppelgänger, Lynch places himself and his own pathologies in the centre of *Blue Velvet*'s mill-wheel; although the film is easily recognisable as absolutely 'personal', MacLachlan's presence (as opposed to, say, the dissimilar and caricatured Jack Nance's in *Eraserhead*) tells us that Lynch knows it as well, and that the film is some form of self-revelation, or self-interrogation. In what way or to what extent, again, we can only guess.

Filled with woods, bugs, coffee, lonely spaces, pop songs drenched with significance and a much-noted admixture of 50s and 80s iconography (Lynch was 17 in 1963, the year Bobby Vinton's rendition of the Bernie Wayne song hit the charts), the movie bursts with its creator's lifestuff, so much so that, a few passages of *Twin Peaks* aside, Lynch could never return convincingly to this turf again, and could never regain the complete confidence, cogency and originality that the film represents.

Home from college (another formative experience for Lynch), to see his hospitalised father (the stricken homeowner with the hose, played by Jack Harvey), Jeffrey is the square-jawed, sweet-tempered, all-American kid, except that he's wearing a black suit and a single gold earring. (Are these indications that Jeffrey is an art student, like Lynch? You're reasonably sure he's not a business administration major.) Jeffrey's initially stunned reaction to what his previously uneventful suburban life has become – an arena of inexplicable cataclysm and lurking secrets – implies that a semester or two away at college was enough to separate the ignorant boy he must have been from the awakening man he is now. Lynch plays out what is effectively the film's first dramatic scene without dialogue: Jeffrey at his father's bedside. He doesn't need dialogue: the daylit image of the red-eyed Mr Beaumont helplessly taped, strapped and screwed into an orthopaedic 'halo', covered with wires and cotton and struggling, whimperingly, with a tracheotomy gate, is a horrific vision of sudden, unfathomable medical collapse, and Jeffrey, like us, is stunned into silence. He takes his father's hand, and eventually must look away from his father's painful efforts – to speak? or is it to clear his throat? to open the gate? Without a word spoken, we are complicit with Lynch's hero, and therefore with Lynch himself.

That Mr Beaumont's illness is never labelled, and that his treatment seems simultaneously both terminally modern and barbarously medieval, is typical of the film's imagistic shorthand. The image of nightmarish hospital gadgetry matters more than the reality of illness or treatment, which is precisely how a child would perceive the scene. The entire film has the aura of being the exaggerated, emotional vision of an innocent – especially later on, in the primal scene between Dorothy Vallens and Frank Booth, where the 'sex' is an occult occurrence we have no key to. In fact, the 'innocent', heavenly touches that Lynch sprinkles throughout the film – Sandy's dream of robins, the romantic dance to the slushy Julee Cruise ballad – are hardly merely 'touches'; they reflect the entire film's subjective, childlike world-view just as the intensive visualisation of mundane matters like hospital rooms, apartment building corridors and sexual encounters does. Horror and hope go hand in hand. Of course, Jeffrey is a teenager, but he still inhabits an unpolluted moral universe at the film's outset – and he is our eyes and ears. (The film's aural impressions are many and complex.) Still, let us not forget that the film is, on the surface, a search for a child (Dorothy's) lost deep in the forest of adult behaviour. No wonder the walls are mauve, and the music drowsingly creepy.

Blue Velvet is, in the profoundest sense, a fairy-tale, a Grimm fable gone literal, American and nervously mad. At this point, Jeffrey is our Alice, on the edge of the rabbit hole, but that's not how it was in Lynch's original conception. According to the original script,[20] a lengthy sequence (much of it shot and later cut) involving Jeffrey at college preceded his hospital visit, including several extraneous scenes involving Jeffrey's college sweetheart and his trip back home. (Like most director-sponsored edits, those made in *Blue Velvet* display astute judgment.) One semi-infamous scene stands out, however: on his way to the lavatory from a school dance, Jeffrey passes by a furnace room and, according to the screenplay, 'is fascinated by a sight, beyond in the darkness'. He's witnessing a date rape in progress, and approaches silently, doing nothing, watching intently. That is, until his steps are heard by the rapist, at which point he intervenes, yelling in typical Lynchian patois, 'Hey, shithead! Leave her alone! Don't force girls!' The loss of this voyeuristic episode, which foreshadows the rest of the film all too clearly, has commonly been lamented by the film's fans, but, like many of the cuts, it preserves the film's suspended, unreal flow. Jeffrey's character hardly required this sort of express clarification; indeed, the film's tone of fierce surprise and trauma, and the vital feeling that the primary events of the film are his first encounter with his own unsavoury impulses, would have been jeopardised with its inclusion.

As it is, Jeffrey's character is truly innocent, a state which implicitly contains the capacity for corruption, the desire for experience. No recourse need be made to 'duality'; though Jeffrey and Frank Booth are (like Dr Treeves and freak 'owner' Bytes in *The Elephant Man*) reflections of one another in a classically Conradian sense, it pays to regard them as points on a sliding scale between virginity and terminal venality rather than opposites. There is no dialectic between them, nor a whole made of halves, merely the struggle of moral balance, which is closely tied to Jeffrey's role as the self-actualising son and Frank's as the evil father.

Walking back from the hospital, Jeffrey pauses to throw rocks at a tin can, and discovers in the grass a severed human ear, crawling with ants. The film seems as startled by this as Jeffrey is and we are: Lynch cuts back and forth between MacLachlan and the mouldering ear no fewer than three times. (Even so, Jeffrey's reaction is essentially childlike, and matter-of-fact.) The ear is the film's launching leitmotif in more ways than one, reoccurring not only as an image (or an absence), but as a channel into the film's aural experience, and its ambiguous status as an internal (psycho-emotional) sequence of events. The ear has, of course, a multiplicity of symbolic meanings, none of which Lynch would ever endorse. 'I don't know why, but it *had* to be an ear,' Lynch has said on more than one occasion.[21] *Why* isn't necessarily a pertinent question; many elements in Lynch's universe simply *are*, as unpredictable facts of nature. We could best consider it as a clue to the hermetic, cloistered logic of the film, where events often happen as if visualised in the head of a dazed pre-adolescent who is *listening* to the inexplicable actions of adults – the pivotal primal scene in Dorothy's apartment is the most crucial example, which we will discuss later. The whole film has the overripe tenor of ardently extrapolated sense knowledge, distorted and amplified by pubertal anxiety and helpless dread.

So, like an overheard secret, the ear is the pass-key to the film's inferno, though at first Jeffrey is pure Hardy Boys: he primly picks the ear up, places it in an old paper-bag and proceeds directly to the Lumberton police station. There, he politely ferrets out a Detective Williams (George Dickerson), who apparently lives near the Beaumonts. Williams is one of the film's great minor inventions, a cosmically suspicious, stern, lizardy, altogether strange cop who seems to have gotten lost on his way to an Anthony Mann noir and wound up in *Our Town*. Whether staring pointlessly at a town wall-map, or wearing his gun holster at home, Williams has his own barely glimpsed edge of perverseness, however much he represents actual, and surprisingly effective, law and order in the film, and Dickerson gives every line reading an extra, discomfiting beat. (He doesn't blink, either.) 'I, uh, found an . . . ear', Jeffrey tells him, holding out the bag. 'You did?' Williams says – amused? 'A human ear?' 'Yeah,' Jeffrey says nervously, 'I thought I should bring it to you.' 'That's right,' Williams muses, opening the bag and waiting a beat. 'Let's just have a look at it.' He peers into the bag for one second too long, then coolly at Jeffrey. 'Yes,' he says, waiting half a beat and smiling, 'that's a human ear, alright.'

Detective Williams embodies what's uniquely hilarious about the whole film: Lynch's inexplicable sense of comic rhythm, which squeezes astonished humour out of the routine moments. Everything is a little off, off from reality *and* off from the rhythms movies usually engender to enfold us into their reality. As a result, we have a special relationship with *Blue Velvet*: half in and half out, half agog and giddy at its off-kilter universe and half creeped out by its alienness, half slave to the narrative's potent liquor and half dazzled spectator. There's little about the film that's not funny – performances, compositions, straight-faced dialogue – and yet it feels like audiovisual trespass, in the deepest personal sense.

From here, the film shorthands the legal aspects of the mystery Whose Ear Is It?, including a trip to the forensics lab, where the lab technician explains that the ear looks like it 'may have been cut off with scissors'. Cut to scissors slicing the 'Police Line' tape, and a distant shot of police combing the field for further clues; Jeffrey paces nearby. Fade to black. When it comes to simply fleshing out the plot's criminal details, Lynch usually skirts the edge of responsibility, and though the plot's gaps and unexplored details have frustrated some literal-minded viewers, they seem to me to be integral to its infantile, panicky flush. A traditional 'complete' mystery would suck the risk away from the more profound mysteries Lynch explores; it would give us a map, a direction, and allow us to overlook the landscape itself.

Like Nancy Drew, the Hardy Boys, the Happy Hollisters and many other teen detectives of mid-century children's literature, Jeffrey finds himself suddenly an amateur sleuth confronting a criminal vortex

I hear you knocking: Jeffrey finds the ear

and discovering quickly that adults will not or cannot come to his aid –
not, at least, to his satisfaction. (The matrix of the Nancy Drew school,
containing provocatively mundane, semi-Lynchian titles like *The Hidden
Staircase* and *The Clue of the Leaning Chimney*, is touched on in many
ways, down to the heroes or heroines almost always having only one
functioning parent.) Blackness gives way to Jeffrey opening his bedroom
door and descending the stairs (by some critics' lights, the ominous
launch into the void), informing his mother (Priscilla Pointer) and
nervous Aunt Barbara (Frances Bay), as they're watching another noirish
koan on TV (from the same perpetual programme?) – this time of feet
walking up a shadowy staircase – that he's taking a walk in the
neighbourhood.

Outside, there follows a typically unexplainably amusing tableau
shot of an enormously fat man standing stock-still in the shadows with a
microscopic dog on a leash. (The dog is so still that you could assume it
was fake – that is, until it turns and looks to Jeffrey as he walks by.) A
small sequence, Jeffrey's first walk into the suburban night, is important
for one reason, outside of Lynch's simple but effective evocation of
menace in the neighbourhood shadows: it is here that Lynch dissolves to
the close-up of the severed ear we've been waiting for, the one that
moves into and through the ear's dark channel the same way Lynch's
camera delved into various abysses in *Eraserhead* and into the pitch of
John Merrick's hood eyehole in *The Elephant Man*. Cut abruptly to
Jeffrey visiting Detective Williams at home – somewhere between the
two houses, Jeffrey (and we) transversed an impasse in the tale, sailing
into the dark space between two ears, a conduit between the then or
there of placid ordinariness and the now or here of peril and dreadful
knowledge. Or is the passage through the ear merely visual punctuation
for a experience that had already begun? Lynch begs the question by
placing the elliptical scene in an otherwise unexceptional narrative
moment – nothing seems to have changed, and Jeffrey learns nothing
new about the ear in his discussion with Williams in his home office. In
any case, we're inside the film's 'head' now. 'Must be great', the curious

Jeffrey says of police work after Williams admonishes him to leave the case to professionals, to which Williams replies – after a pregnant half-beat – 'It's horrible, too.'

We think we're close to understanding what he means, but we truly have no idea, not yet. Neither does Jeffrey, who exits the Williams home with a 'Say hello to Sandy for me'. (The Williams house is significantly larger and more affluent than the Beaumonts' – the classist span between the two resonates in Williams's condescending regard for Jeffrey, and in the implicit crisis, explicit in the original screenplay, that Mr Beaumont's illness may financially squelch Jeffrey's freshman college career. Then again, Mrs Williams (Hope Lange) and Mrs Beaumont are nearly identical – a great visual joke at the film's denouement.) Sandy herself (Laura Dern) has a smashing entrance: as Jeffrey nears the sidewalk, a voice asks him, 'Are you the one who found the ear?' He turns, Lynch cuts to unfocused shadow, and the golden-haired Sandy slowly emerges into the light. Like so much in the film, Sandy has the aura of an archetype: the pure-hearted, kind, suburban high-school girl (though obviously bra-less – a detail akin to Jeffrey's earring) with whom a classic hero could eventually find solace, love and sanctuary away from the chaos of the world at large after his external and internal battles are done. In an oedipal context, she's the nurturing girl the hero will return to after struggling with his parental alliances and attaining self-possession, and indeed Jeffrey does, but with a subtly Lynchian difference.

Sandy and Jeffrey walk in the evening, chatting initially about the ear; Sandy has overheard from her father's office that the case might have something to do with a 'singer', Dorothy Vallens, who lives at a nearby sleazy apartment building, on the seventh floor. 'It's a strange world, isn't it?' Jeffrey sighs in one of the film's memorable and gratifying signature lines (and what could've easily been its promo blurb), as Lynch cuts to a view of the dark overhead trees passing them as they walk. Having the apartment building so close by is what's 'creepy' to Sandy, though this hardly stops her from showing it to Jeffrey

Gaining experience: Jeffrey delivers the ear to Detective Williams (George Dickerson), and moving in on Sandy (Laura Dern)

– Lynch telegraphs the mood by scanning its unlit windows and fire escapes, and panning to the street sign, LINCOLN, in portentous close-up. (Is the confluence of the street name and the last name Booth coincidental in a town haunted by the ghost of a fading lumber industry?[22]) Again, it's all done in the visual vocabulary of a startled child. The maintenance of this viewpoint could easily seem clumsy in other hands, but Lynch, like Charles Laughton before him in *The Night of the Hunter*, handles it with an effortless and flawless instinctual wisdom. Recall other Hollywood attempts at stylising a child's perspectives – even semi-successful forays into pop expressionism like William Cameron Menzies's *Invaders from Mars* (1953) and Robert Wise/Val Lewton's *Curse of the Cat People* (1944) – and it's apparent how easily the concept can become unruly and absurd. Lynch's sensibility is never excessive, and is thoroughly grounded in a contrasting orthodoxy, against which his lurid topos seems all the stranger. Restraint is as vital to his movie as the infamous extravagances.

A sound indication of the degree to which the ambience of Lynch's universe is so successfully contrived is that we often don't know *why* it works – a simple shot of a street sign or a staircase or wind-blown trees is just enough, at that moment, to establish moods and subconscious connections within the film we couldn't hope to fully account for. It's a poetical logic, and it cannot be profitably flow-charted or imitated. Moreover, the unbreakable beauty of the film resides in the fact that nearly every scene is a diagram of the film as a whole – you can extrapolate the film's entirety from any individual setpiece.

An ostensible 'innocent' like Jeffrey, Sandy seems just as prone as he is to sticking her nose where it doesn't belong; still, she's infinitely more sensible and in control of her drives. They continue to walk and establish a rapport, Jeffrey cracking Sandy up with non-sequitur bits of business like remembering a kid who 'had the biggest tongue in the world', and performing, apropos of nothing, a hunched 'chicken walk' for her. This scene, as harmless as it is, comes closest to the subsequent non-sequitur ramblings of *Wild at Heart* and *Fire Walk with Me* than anything else in the movie; all told, they suggest that rather than straining for *Blue Velvet*'s oddness in subsequent films, Lynch may be indulging a current of free-associative subconscious logic no one else has access to. Given the intense, private nature of the material we can read, we shouldn't be at all surprised.

The next day, in the hardware store Mr Beaumont owns, Jeffrey is gearing up some bug-spraying equipment, and swaps banter with two black and ageing store employees, one blind, both called jointly Double Ed. Their house-slave fawning, post-vaudeville manner and lack of individual identity comes close to a cozy caricature, reminiscent of old Hollywood stereotypes. The quasi-50s feel continues with Jeffrey pulling up outside the high school in a red convertible to pick up Sandy, who, like all her friends, wears a long skirt, sweater and flat shoes – Natalie Wood in *Rebel without a Cause* looks trampy by comparison. At the town diner they have Cokes and fries. You expect Troy Donahue to turn up in a varsity sweater and play some Bill Haley on the jukebox. The film's popularly noted collocation of 50s and 80s iconography, beyond its placing the film's action in a social (and personal, for Lynch) void, suggests a sense of similarity between the two decades that directly addresses Lynch's much-professed interest at the time in the Reagan administration, also in its way a socio-political titan with a foot in each decade. In both cases, the 60s and 70s are contexts which do not need to be and are not addressed. In America, the 50s and 80s were both marked by surging affluence, stalwart conservatism and rampaging conformism; it's clear that, astonishing as it initially seems, Lynch is essentially conformist in principles. How he expresses those principles is another matter: he stumps for orthodoxy by exploring its antithesis. His sympathies straddle the divide between Jeffrey's and Frank's worlds; he champions one while indulging his fascination and empathy with the other.

'There are opportunities in life for gaining knowledge and experience; sometimes it's necessary to take a risk.' So Jeffrey introduces his plan, on the scantiest of evidence, to infiltrate Dorothy Vallens's apartment and 'sneak in, hide and observe'. Since Lynch hardly cares enough for the logical realities of police work and plot to make the connection between Vallens and the ear – however vaguely overheard by Sandy – concrete, we shouldn't be too surprised that Jeffrey, the director's idealised self, doesn't care either. He's simply slaking his thirst for dark knowledge. His leap into the ethical void here is the first solid indication we get that Jeffrey is not quite Andy Hardy, but it's hardly a shock. He says as much himself, pace William Blake: the nature of innocence is to lust for experience, knowledge (and self-knowledge) cannot remain in stasis, growth is painful and terrifying as well as inevitable and necessary. In addition, the reasoning Jeffrey uses is as infantile as the film's traumatised sensuousness – he's like a child longing to stick a fork into an electrical socket, just to see what happens. It's a transparently sexual urge, and therefore one that translates, oedipally, to a hunger for self-realisation. It's not that Jeffrey has a 'dark side', as has been often noted; *Blue Velvet* is a wrenching dramatisation of psychosexual maturation in an abstracted, universal sense. Lynch is using his internal experience to express our own.

Sneak in, hide and observe; it's as if he's *looking* for a primal scene, to see his parents enact the forbidden ritual of sex. ('A little nightmare about the fear connected with learning' is how Lynch described his early short *The Alphabet*.[23]) Jeffrey offers a scheme involving the two of them masquerading as a pest-control man and a Jehovah's Witness – two rather parasitic, fringy social figures – so Jeffrey can gain access and unlock a window to crawl into later. 'It sounds like a good daydream, but ... it's too weird,' Sandy worries, to which Jeffrey reasons, 'No one will suspect us!' She admits he's got a point, and off they go.

Outfitted in work coveralls and an old-fashioned bugspray tank, Jeffrey enters the Deep River Apartments through the lobby, an only marginally more civilised area than the lobby of Henry's building in *Eraserhead*, complete with perpetually buzzing neon sign (unseeable, if not inaudible, on the videotape version of the film – few 80s films took such advantage of the wide CinemaScope frame), green-grey walls and an out-of-service antique lift. In the original screenplay, an elderly woman confronts Jeffrey here, proclaiming 'Well, it's about *time* you came!', suggesting the Deep River has a predictably serious bug problem. (Jeffrey was to mutter to himself in reply, 'That's a good sign'; you can easily imagine hearing MacLachlan whisper this perfect bit of straight-faced Lynchian nonsense.) The outside stairs to the Deep River are a windy, desolate affair, resounding with the subindustrial echoes of the place (what Kael said sounded like 'a heavy old animal that's winded'[24]). Upstairs, the tonal scheme of the Deep River building – a fungoid, shitty green – and the expansive framing (Lynch was using a new telescopic, wide-angle lens that takes in vast interiors without warping) jack the film's idiosyncratic visual substance into a new realm.

In Dorothy's kitchen with the faux bug spray

Hardly the cartoon tableaux from the beginning, nor the prosaically framed presentation of the suburban world outside, the Deep River is a world unto itself, and possesses an altogether clammy, subterranean character that so superbly invokes the actual experience of outdated, decaying, trashy American living spaces that your skin can crawl without even considering its subtextual gist. 'Deep River' indeed; this is definitely Lumberton's heart of darkness, the reservoir of its guilt, hate and despair. Moreover, it's an essentially 'adult' environment – children who live there get kidnapped or abused, and Jeffrey is from the start wholly out of his element. Less literally, it's a locus for sexual activity as perceived by a child, a place (like a parental bedroom) where grown-ups do unpleasant, unsavoury, painful-sounding things to each other that we cannot fathom. Here is where Lynch's love for resonant details explodes: the Deep River is a secret closet overflowing with adult objects that can fill a naive kid with obscure nausea; Dorothy's velvet bathrobe and formless wig, the sleazy whorehouse furniture, the ugly, short-circuiting fluorescent lights, even the stark, strangely unplantlike snake plants scattered throughout Dorothy's apartment (which, Lynch may have known, are one of the few common houseplants that can survive with next to no sunlight – perfect for the Deep River – and which were cheaply fashionable in the 50s).

When Jeffrey knocks on the apartment door, we get our first glimpse of Dorothy (Isabella Rossellini) – as a harried eye peering through an open crack in the bolted door. The rhythm of this scene is sharply comical: 'Pest control. Gotta do your apartment,' Jeffrey says, at which Dorothy groans, slams the door and, after half a beat, unlocks it and lets him in. 'That stuff stinks,' Dorothy says. 'This is new stuff,' Jeffrey says calmly. 'There's no smell.'

Darkly European, heavily made-up, vaguely anxious, lounging around her ill-decorated apartment in a flimsy scarlet lounge dress and a sluttish wig, Dorothy is another archetype, or rather, several twisted into one unhappy knot. Down to her druggy cabaret act, she's an ageing harlot and classic Jocasta figure, a forbidden yet frighteningly available mother figure seen purely in terms of seductive dread. At the same time, she's a pathetic victim, a wife and mother disoriented, whored and edged into sadomasochistic psychopathy by her circumstances, and longing for a release through death. (More on this later.) She's even more of a child in some ways than Jeffrey, though the same could be said of Frank Booth. Jeffrey seems simultaneously attracted and repulsed by her (Freud's taboo-related emotional ambivalence), and yet is moved beyond all other things to save her. Her crucible is his; by suturing the fissures in her life and psyche, he becomes a man.

Jeffrey has perhaps only the merest glimmerings of this dynamic as yet, however much he plans to enter this taboo zone later and secretly watch its inhabitants perform their mysteries without knowledge of being seen – a near-perfect definition of voyeurism as a sexual disorder. As he apes spraying Dorothy's kitchen (laid out and lit like a crummy department store display from the 50s), another knock is heard ('Grand Central Station', Dorothy kvetches), but it's not Sandy – it's the Yellow Man (Fred Pickler), a fat, suspicious-looking man in a yellow blazer, whom Dorothy knows. 'It's only the bug man,' she tells him. He and Jeffrey lock sightlines, and he leaves. In the meantime, Jeffrey steals a key (oddly kept on a hook under the kitchen counter) and finishes up spraying (marking his territory?), exiting shyly. He meets Sandy on the stairs, who explains that she was usurped in her role at Dorothy's door by the approach of the Yellow Man.

The role of the Yellow Man in *Blue Velvet*'s fabric, as well as *why yellow?*, is far from clear; even on a fundamentally literal level, we're never sure what role he's had in the kidnapping of Dorothy's husband and the climactic criminal fall-out we see in the end. We do learn that he's a cop, apparently corrupt, but working in close quarters to Detective Williams. Other than that, he's merely one of many tangential elements of the Frank Booth plot, which we know only fragments of by the film's end – after all, our role, like Jeffrey's, is that of a naive observer with no access to the whole, objective truth of what happens. We only know what haphazardly enters our field of experience, however we, like Jeffrey, endeavour to see things we shouldn't; often what we see is only the consequence and aftermath of the 'plot'. As with the police work initially done on the severed ear, Lynch shorthands the nuts and bolts of action narrative; when the police confront Frank Booth and his crew in a gory shoot-out, we see only glimpses of the battle intercut with Jeffrey in Dorothy's apartment and scored to Ketty Lester crooning 'Love Letters'. What happened isn't important; what it means is.

Back downstairs and in Jeffrey's red-hot convertible, Sandy and Jeffrey review what happened and plan for more, eventually (after some deliberations by Sandy concerning her football-playing boyfriend Mike) deciding to meet that night at an interstate dive called The Slow Club, where, as Sandy overheard, Dorothy Vallens works as a chanteuse. At the club, Jeffrey and Sandy enjoy a few Heinekens waiting for the show, in classic Lynchian cadences: after proclaiming his love for the ubiquitous Dutch import, Sandy replies she's never tasted it before. 'My father drinks Bud,' she says by way of explanation. Jeffrey nods. 'King of beers,' he muses. MacLachlan treats this scene with the same gravity he shows throughout his quite amazing and underrated performance, but it's the film's amused-Martian take on American beer culture that's truly hilarious: the vectors of masculine tension tug between the open-minded/semi-cultured Heineken lover, the authoritarian Budweiser disciple and the blisteringly chaotic white-trash Pabst devotee, Frank Booth ('Heineken?! FUCK THAT SHIT!! Pabst! Blue! Ribbon!'). *Blue Velvet* is, in its own idiosyncratic way, a very class-conscious film, thoroughly involved with the anxiety of bourgeois stasis in the face of an irrational and unappeasable underclass. Between them, the blue-collar middle class strives to mend the rift and, in the process, discover itself.

Dorothy is no mean class symbol herself, making her living as a singer in a north-western roadhouse, her life and family decimated by a secret interface with poverty and violence. All the same, she remains a strange, glowing vision of maternal ambiguity; even The Slow Club is an enigma, with its stylised, dreary quasi-jazz stage show eagerly taken in by its Middle American, uneducated lumbertown patrons. (In reality, or a

normal movie, the band would be playing Marshall Tucker covers.)
Lynch's repeated close-ups of MacLachlan's awed face (and Dern's
discomfited squirmings) reveal this to be an epiphany of serious
proportions – it's Jeffrey's first interface with sexual spectacle, with the
danger of desire. (Consider as well another notorious cut image shot in
the bar: that of an obese topless dancer in the background lighting her
breasts on fire – Lynch eventually thought it too obtrusive to the
foreground dialogue.[25]) In a classically Freudian sense, this is his first
sexual thought, the first awakening of lust for the mother. Dorothy
represents the sexual force of the mother because she is forbidden and
because she becomes the object of the unhealthy, infantile impulses at
work in Jeffrey's subconscious. (And Lynch's? A Lynch/Rossellini
relationship did emerge after the shooting of the film – the one film in

Dorothy hits
the boards at the
Slow Club

which the world-famous supermodel was deliberately made to look as
unappealing as possible.)

The scene indeed seems tinted by Jeffrey's stunned longing:
slouching in a velvet dress that looks like it was poured out of a syrup
bottle, tonelessly moaning 'Blue Velvet' into an antique microphone and
drenched in blue light, Dorothy is the apotheosis of the cheap mysteries
of sex, or rather, sex as it's conceived in popular culture, as the

heightened province of masculine want. Dorothy is an empty vessel into which Jeffrey's desires cascade; his controlling 'gaze' is so direct and pivotal it's almost a parody of feminist theorising, except that we can safely assume Lynch entertained no such political strategies. In fact, Dorothy's role in the film as a literal victim of male fantasies – even Jeffrey's – neatly transforms the familiar theoretical apparatus into real thematic dough. Dorothy is never less than idealised (in as many ways as there are male characters, but she's never objectified as a sex object for the viewer), her primary struggle is with those idealisations; she must wrestle and negotiate with them to find both her missing child and her restored self-worth as a mother.

It's fitting that immediately after Dorothy's set, Jeffrey decides that night to sneak into her apartment; his reasons are still vaguely

In the closet

degenerate, prompting a still-wary Sandy to say, 'I don't know if you're a detective or a pervert.' It's a more-than-fair question; a smiling Jeffrey responds in vintage playground lingo: 'That's for me to know and you to find out.' They contrive a warning system (Sandy will beep the car horn when Dorothy comes home), and off he goes.

Here we enter the movie's burial chamber, the centre of its pyramid. Accompanied by the accentuation of, via Alan Splet's trademarked sonic 'design', the Deep River's underworldly rumble and cough, Jeffrey makes his surreptitious way upstairs, down the hallway and into Dorothy's room. In the darkness, he examines the dishevelled rooms (one obviously a nursery), and eventually discovers the bathroom, where he feels free to relieve his beer-bloated bladder. ('Heineken', he sighs.) Unfortunately, Dorothy arrives downstairs, and Sandy lets loose with her warning beeps just as Jeffrey flushes the extraordinarily loud toilet. Hearing Dorothy enter, Jeffrey quickly improvises and dashes into the black closet, his view of the room thereafter provided by the slats of the louvred closet door.

We're never sure Jeffrey would've paid any attention to Sandy's warning anyway – once in the apartment, he's in a dreamy daze, not looking for clues so much as satisfying a thirst, even pausing after he zips up to fondle a tchotchke in Dorothy's bathroom. He's a child rummaging through the strange, sexually active spaces of his mother, distracted from the suspenseful situation at hand just as he is later very easily distracted from the real criminal crisis – the kidnapping of Dorothy's husband and child – in favour of Dorothy's carnal vulnerability and psychological confusion. As he looks through the door at Dorothy desultorily undressing, it's apparent he's not worried at this point about the severed ear, or even being caught – he's in the seductive grip of a taboo. The phone rings, and instantly the semi-naked Dorothy scrambles for it, her voice running through about three different registers as she pleads with someone named Frank – remembering to call him 'sir' only after he reminds her – and begs to speak to her missing husband ('Don'), who apparently is too beaten and delirious to make any sense. 'You mean Madeleine?' Dorothy asks in an apparent non-sequitur (though a foreshadow to *Twin Peaks*, and therefore a hearkening backward to the dreamy blonde/brunette dichotomy of Hitchcock's *Vertigo*), and then screams in a panic, 'Frank, what's the *matter* with him?'

And finally: 'Mommy loves you,' she says to Frank in an obedient murmur; this brief scene is like the delirious one-woman show of a Doris Lessing novel, and Rossellini, already fragmenting before our eyes, keeps us always one step short of knowing what's precisely going on on the other end. After hanging up, Jeffrey silently observes her examining a framed picture she keeps under the sofa, taking her wig off, stalking down the hallway to the bathroom, returning wrapped in a towel and with her wig back on. This time she goes straight for the closet, and Jeffrey quickly hides in the shadows as she grabs her blue velvet robe and puts it on, sitting still and waiting . . . for something. Then Jeffrey makes a noise, and she hears it.

When Dorothy finally throws open the closet door – with a butcher knife gripped tightly in her right hand and a chilling Badalamenti blast on the soundtrack – the passive nature of Jeffrey's deviance is plunged into an arena of involvement and hot truth he's completely unprepared for. Shrieking commands at him – 'Hands behind your head! Kneel down!' – Dorothy manages to behave like an ordinary outraged woman for a time, and Jeffrey, though terrified, still thinks he can back out of it like a kid who's jumped the wrong fence. Even after she suddenly jabs the knife into his cheek ('What's your name?!' 'Jeffrey.' 'Jeffrey who?' 'Jeffrey Nothing.' Jab), Jeffrey still has a grip on the sociosexual handrail. 'I sprayed your apartment,' he admits to her, 'I stole your keys, I didn't mean to do anything but see you.' 'Do you always sneak into girls' apartments to watch them get undressed?' Dorothy hisses, not unreasonably, and Jeffrey answers, with puppy-dog eyes, 'Never before this.'

'I only wanted to see you,' he repeats, and he's not lying. When she commands him to get undressed, the knife shaking in the air the whole time ('Please, just let me leave,' he pleads; 'NO WAY!' she rasps,

(overleaf) The primal scene turned purple: Frank (Dennis Hopper) and Dorothy act out their warped pas de deux as both Jeffrey and we watch from the shadows

'I want to see you GET UNDRESSED!'), both we and Jeffrey know all bets are off – welcome to the jungle of tortured sexual aberration. Jeffrey strips, and Dorothy pulls down his boxers (knife still in hand – as an expression of castration anxiety, this scene comes close to *Goldfinger* and *Ms. 45*, though a few slashes shy of *In the Realm of the Senses* or *I Spit on Your Grave*). Dorothy suddenly becomes flushed with lust, kissing Jeffrey's abdomen and leg, eventually going down on him. 'Do you like that?' 'Yes,' he whispers intensely, hardly the mere spectator any more. Suddenly she lashes out: 'Don't move! Don't look at me!' Another oasis of cozy, oral ardour is interrupted by 'Don't touch me or I'll kill you!' followed immediately, softly, by 'Do you like talk like that?'

'No,' a frazzled Jeffrey whispers. We understand soon enough that the sadistic fetishism is not in fact Dorothy's – it's Frank's – and she is enacting the abuse heaped upon her as if it is her sole sexual experience, like a child who tortures animals after being abused by his or her parents. There's little reason to suspect her marriage suffered from a similar psychopathology. Once we see, as Jeffrey does, Frank's sadomasochistic ritual in full swing, however, it's easy to understand Dorothy's disorientation. Repeatedly forced into the role of masochistic mother-whore by Frank, she ping-pongs between natural sexual warmth and violent habit when confronted with a normal, willing partner.

Jeffrey, of course, never dreamed that sex – the essence, truly, of what differentiates the adult and infantile worlds – would ever be like this: terrifying, paralysing, chaotic beyond understanding, fuelled by impulses so chthonic they seem unreal, paranormal, spiritually diseased. In the end, it'd be too easy to summarise this sequence, or the entire film, as a symbolic crucible Jeffrey must pass through on his way to sexual maturity; there's no room in such an admittedly convenient reading for the unprecedented imagining and bone-deep disquiet Lynch brings to the film's notion of psychological disorder. The whole scenario from Dorothy's sputtering seduction of Jeffrey to Frank's ghastly performance – a shrieking, algolagnic compound of frottage, rape, sadism, torture, fetishistic obsession, helpless incestuous anxiety, delusion and infantile rage – is a sexual dynamic several steps beyond the diagnostic potentialities of DSM-III or other conventional psychoanalytic measurements, and therefore, perhaps, beyond our experience. It is an extremity of imagined human behaviour, a submersion in infernal appetites.

At Dorothy's command, the two move to the couch – Dorothy holding the knife up like Mrs Bates the whole time – and begin to make love, when a knock on the door sends Dorothy into a frenzied panic. 'Don't say anything,' she tells Jeffrey, stuffing him back into the closet, 'he'll kill you, I mean it!' It's a moment echoing with cliché – though she's superficially hiding a lover from a jealous husband, Dorothy is more accurately a battered wife scrambling to please her abusive mate. Returned to his relatively safe, voyeuristic preadolescent stronghold in the closet, Jeffrey watches the action, as we do, and we're never not aware of his presence.

The 'Dad' in question is Frank Booth (Dennis Hopper), and it's with him that the film's engagement of its themes becomes action rather than thought. Frank is an all-purpose sociopath, a raging, seizing, uncontrollable juggernaut of libidinal will and hate. The more we know about Frank's ferocious hungers and paraphiliac impulses, the less we can predict them, and though he certainly stands as one of the most horrifying characters in film history, he is nonetheless torturously, miserably human. In Lynch's and Hopper's hands, the most appalling acts of debasement and viciousness have a edge of sad struggle to them, as if Frank is striving toward a satisfaction he can never attain – like an abandoned infant. His tantrums incorporate many defences typical of borderline personalities: splitting, idealisation, projection, fantasies of omnipotence, identity diffusion and rage about dependency.[26] Between Frank, Dorothy and Jeffrey, *Blue Velvet* digs at a primordial truth about human emotional need, the horrified frustrations that plague us if our needs are not met, and the subterranean knots those frustrations bind up inside of us. In this world, the pure anger of a neglected baby can poison the very air.

So, perhaps Dorothy isn't merely a skittish masochist and victim – though her guilt about not being able to rescue her son would be reason enough, given a fragile ego. Perhaps she recognises the agonised infant inside of Frank, and realises that whatever traumas induced his pain may very well be occurring to her own son at this moment. Her acquiescent role as the defiled 'mommy' in Frank's gnashing psychodrama may be her half-conscious way of trying to prevent the generation of a new Frank Booth.

As far as Jeffrey's concerned, however, what ensues at this moment is a primal scene unlike any other in film, or psychoanalytic, history, and he's the tyro illegally observing his parents. 'Hello, baby,' Dorothy says mechanically as Frank scans the room disapprovingly. 'Shut up! It's Daddy, you shithead! Where's my bourbon?!' he bellows. 'Can't

In mid-quasi-rape, Frank responds to unseen demons

you fucking remember anything?' She turns down the light, lights a candle on the wall. 'Now it's dark,' Frank murmurs. Everything has the air of strained ritual. They sit across from each other. 'Spread your legs,' he says, and drinks his bourbon with a savoury gesture. 'Don't you fucking look at me!' he spits, and Dorothy's head lolls back, facing up to the ceiling. Then he gets out his gas mask.

The gas in question was originally conceived by Lynch as helium, which would do little more for Frank than make his voice shrilly preadolescent, thereby augmenting his own oedipal scenario. According to Hopper in various interviews,[27] he convinced Lynch – after some trials – that the effect would be more comical than disturbing. Hopper, bearing a notoriously encyclopedic knowledge of substance abuse, suggested nitrous oxide, which would aggravate and accelerate Frank's

Exit Frank; Jeffrey emerges from safety to become an active participant in Dorothy's psychodrama

already wicked state of mind. Lynch apparently went with Hopper's idea, in which Frank gets jacked up on laughing gas and mewls like a horny dog, although according to *Video Watchdog*, Hopper revealed in a TV interview years later a laggardly appreciation for Lynch's original conception, and admitted to being curious of how it might've played as written. The mind boggles, but as it is, Frank's delirious gas ravings are effective and potent.

He kneels before Dorothy, staring at her exposed crotch, sucking in gas like a baby on a teat (together, the mask and his black leather outfit invoke the beetles from the beginning), whining 'Mommy, mommy! . . . Baby wants to *fuck*!' He glances around him, as if hallucinating – 'Get away you fucks!' – catches Dorothy looking at him and slams her. 'Don't you fucking look at me!'

'Baby wants blue velvet,' he mutters in a fetishy pant, and Dorothy, on cue, tucks a piece of her robe into his mouth, provoking a swoony moan. In the mock-rape, amphetaminic hump that ensues, Frank switches from 'baby' mode to full-fledged 'Daddy' mode, proclaiming 'Daddy's coming home!' But, instead of raping her, he roughly jams pieces of her robe between her legs; Frank seems to be, for all intents and purposes, impotent. As Lynne Layton pointed out, although 'fuck' seems to be every other word out of his mouth, it's the one thing he seems incapable of doing.[28] When he does hump her, he does it like a crazed beast – we never again see him so helpless, so unhappy. He consequently suffers what looks like a sex/drug-induced apoplexy, jerking his hand out as if to try to regain control of it. When he's finished, he stands over the prone Dorothy like a playground bully. 'Now it's dark,' he says again, blowing out the candle (a mantra reportedly improvised by Hopper).

In this one scene (which seems to last an hour, but is in fact only five minutes), Frank's psychopathology is so vivid, so palpable we can taste it, even if we cannot in fact understand it completely. His role as the corrupt Daddy alternates with his re-enactment of his own oedipal trauma, and his rage at not finding his bourbon ready for him at the outset suggests that he cannot understand how everyone else fails to grasp the importance and position of each role. At the same time, as *Cahiers du cinéma* critic Michel Chion has pointed out in his fine monograph on Lynch,[29] the scenario is just as much psychodramatic playlet as ritual – both participants act as if they're bad actors in a low-rent chamber piece, stumbling through their lines as the Slutty Mother and Brutish Father. This suggests several levels of subtext: that Jeffrey, watching quietly in the dark, is us the audience, and movies are our collective 'primal scenes', and that the forced dialogue of the scene, the bizarre and impotent mockery of sex it portrays, and the fearsome weirdness of Frank's chaotic utterances, smacks of the scrambling, terrified images conjured by a child *listening* to his parents making love. However much visual voyeurism is involved, it's still the ear as agent of mystery and disinformation that dominates the film. And however much Jeffrey is experiencing the primal scene as a loaded series of childish misinterpretations, it's clear that, since the psychodrama in question is in fact 'scripted' by Frank, that it's *his* primal scene we're witnessing, or more exactly, its re-enactment. Frank's subconscious suffering is so strong that, for the moments he's on screen, *Blue Velvet* is his feverdream, not Jeffrey's. Later, when we and Jeffrey spot him watching Dorothy sing the titular song at The Slow Club, he's fondling a piece of velvet and crying – his vicious rituals are the product of memories he cannot exorcise in any other manner. The film pulses with empathy for Frank's internal dilemma; nearly every scene is the by-product of his tortures.

After Frank exits, Jeffrey crawls from the closet and attempts to comfort Dorothy – 'I don't like that,' she snaps. Dorothy's masochistic role in the film is a troubled one; she never seems sure of what she wants or why, and the continuing trauma inflicted upon her by Frank doesn't simply create a perversity, it agitates Dorothy into a schizophrenic chaos. Despite her dangerous state of mind, Jeffrey seems intent on providing succour – and taking adolescent advantage of a sexually vulnerable situation – and indeed the two get intimate.

Dorothy's initial proclamation 'Don, hold me!' should've sent up some warning flags, but by this point Jeffrey's sensible college student identity has receded and his oedipal role as hormonally driven motherfucker has taken over.

All the same, Dorothy's manipulative attempts to seduce Jeffrey only work until she asks, then insists, that he hit her. Lynch shoots Rossellini in a monstrous upside-down close-up, her lips glistening as she purrs, 'Hit me!' Jeffrey, only ready to go so far along in his pursuit, begs off. 'I'm leaving now,' he says to her after he's gotten dressed. 'Don't,' she whispers into the bathroom sink. 'Help me.'

The reverberations from his evening spent in oedipal horror/lust never truly leave Jeffrey, just as a primal scene, witnessed so acutely, can linger over one's subconscious life for decades. After a fierce dream sequence (in which Jeffrey sees *himself* for a moment as Dorothy, pummelled by Frank), Jeffrey wakes up with a start, and Lynch slowly pans up the bedroom wall to an unspecified object hanging on a nail: an amorphous brown rubber shape, seemingly a deflated balloon or toy, whose distinguishing characteristic is a yawning mouth lined with teeth. Though the significance of this little totem is truly up for grabs, we can read the ambiguous strangeness of it as echoing Jeffrey's feelings of guilt and unease.

In any case, Jeffrey's light-hearted, adventure-seeking demeanour is no more – compare his transformation to the embarrassed giggles of the sexually inactive teenager giving way to the impassioned gravity of the newly initiated – and Sandy notices immediately. Parking in Jeffrey's car the next evening outside a warmly lit church, Jeffrey gives Sandy the facts of the matter, leaving out the sordid and incriminating details:

Dorothy Vallens is married to a man named Don. They have a son. I think that the son and husband have been kidnapped by a man named Frank. Frank has done this to force Dorothy to do things for him. I think she wants to die. I think Frank cut the ear I found off her husband as a warning to her to stay alive.

Jeffrey's conclusions are based almost wholly on one moment, Frank's departing declaration to Dorothy: 'You're still alive, baby. Do it for Van Gogh.' If the Dorothy–Frank dynamic makes sense outside of its collision of deviant needs and psychological battery, it may pivot on this one reading. Chion thinks so, maintaining that 'Dorothy is prey to a sense of terminal depression', and that Frank's scheme (whatever its untold literal aspects) revolves around keeping Dorothy alive by threatening her with the lives of her family. Frank's thesis here is far from clear, but Dorothy's becomes lucid. As Chion points out, not only does Dorothy fit the paradigm of Lynch heroines from Mary in *Eraserhead* to Laura Palmer in *Twin Peaks*, her behaviour throughout is that of a forestalled suicide. The help she requests from Jeffrey has apparently nothing to do with her kidnapped family; she needs to be

Dorothy at the Slow

saved from slipping into a void and never coming out. Jeffrey realises
this immediately, although he understands as little as we do as to why
she is as she is. (Lynch had shot and then cut a scene on the Deep River
roof, where Dorothy explains to Jeffrey that it's where she means to
jump to her death; she then complains about a fear of falling.) It's as if
Dorothy, so submerged into her quasi-Jocasta role for Frank and now
Jeffrey, is mourning her husband before he has even been killed.
Dorothy could also simply be a vision of womanhood as Lynch perceives
it – sexually maddened and perpetually on the edge of dissolution. Laura
Palmer was framed in a similarly Romantic/surrealist fashion. Feminist
theory – of which a great deal has been written on Lynch and *Blue Velvet*
– favours this view, that Dorothy's manipulation by the film's men is
equal to her manipulation by the film-maker, and that her 'enjoyment' of
violence allows the typical masculine 'gaze' to enjoy it as well, guilt-free,
as pleasurable visual stimulus. Perhaps, but if only, as Jane M. Shattuc
points out,[30] *Blue Velvet* was a typical Hollywood film, and if only we
could so conveniently equate, in feminist theory's grand way, the
interrogatable 'pleasure' of cinematic viewership (in *Blue Velvet*'s case,
Dorothy's assaults are far from fun) with a cinematic moment's
'meaning'. In any case, *Blue Velvet* is a Gordian knot of political
readings; because it deals in semi-pure Lynch-stuff, and less in the world
at large, every thread of its web can be interpreted according to your
wants. Besides, though Jeffrey's gaze dominates the film, it's a gaze that
de-eroticises the female form even as it longs for its idealisation, a
process closely tied to the experience of emotional maturation. Jeffrey,
after all, comes to understand Dorothy's 'gaze' by becoming the object
of Frank's assault (sexual and otherwise), and he locates little enjoyment
in it.

'You found out all of this in one night?' Sandy gasps when Jeffrey
finishes. 'It *is* a strange world.' She doesn't know the half of it, and
Jeffrey shows no signs of wanting to tell her. He's right not to, as we
more fully understand when Sandy suddenly says 'I had a dream ...',
and launches into her Blakean vision of empyrean wonder, an epiphany

scored with liturgical organ moans. 'In the dream, our world was dark because there weren't any robins . . .' she exalts, enjoying her vision of a descending flood of robins and love on to a darkling plain. 'I guess it means there's trouble 'til the robins come.' Like Laura Palmer, Sandy is a Lynchian paradigm of conceptualised goodness, so pure it's sort of weird, and in both instances the films around them reverberate with heartsickness over their inevitable confrontation with the destructive forces of the world. Lynch doesn't bleed in the same manner for Jeffrey; his is a rite of passage he must endure. You get the sense from *Blue Velvet* and *Twin Peaks* that Lynch in his heart would like to save the sweet, blonde homecoming queen from having to grow up, from having to be corrupted, to age, to lose her innocent bloom. It's Lynch's greatest tragedy (nothing is quite as genuinely felt in either *Eraserhead* or *Wild at Heart*), and at the same time he recognises the inexorability and complexity of experience. In this rather politically unpopular way, he is an intensely conservative storyteller, a consort of J.M. Barrie.

Immediately after meeting Sandy, Jeffrey returns to Dorothy's apartment (at which point comes the immortal line 'I looked for you in my closet tonight') to make love to her. The film then shifts into exposition overdrive, with Jeffrey tracking Frank down after a night at The Slow Club, staking him out all night in the run-down industrial parts of town, meeting Sandy the next day and eagerly apprising her of his new findings at the local diner. None of Jeffrey's discoveries (which include a cartoonishly staged crime scene 'in the distance' involving drug dealers) add up to anything comprehensible, a scheme of Lynch's that may frustrate in the initial viewing, but subsequently seems utterly rational. Jeffrey, after all, is a harrowed kid tagging after monstrous adults, and to provide him with enough information to make sense of things would be to betray his character and how it's affected by the story's elliptical events.

'I'm seeing something that was always hidden,' he explains to a wary Sandy in another hopelessly quotable tag line. 'I'm involved in a mystery – I'm *in the middle* of a mystery. And it's all secret.' That's the whole movie, and – at least in terms of *Blue Velvet* and its tamer, relatively self-indulgent TV cousin *Twin Peaks* – it's Lynch's whole aesthetic, down to the expression of sex-fear, the acknowledgment of oedipal self-hate, the parental qualm, the political tensions (what do the middle class *truly* know about the troglodytes, anyway?), even down to the unknowable degree to which Lynch's own life is the source of the film's basic materials. What *Blue Velvet* gives us that lasts long after the shock and laughter have faded is its vibrant evocation of a secret history, both personal and social, literal and psychological. Its mysteries are unsolvable, but we never feel frustrated by withheld answers or wilful obscurity, as patient viewers of *Twin Peaks*'s second season were. The mysteries here are universally sensed and everlastingly indecipherable. Jeffrey even woos Sandy a little by flatly saying, 'You're a mystery.' She is, of course, no less than Dorothy or Frank, no less than the Deep River, The Slow Club or the ear. No less, certainly, than Lynch himself, at least as we know him through his work.

When Jeffrey returns to Dorothy's apartment for a second tryst – neatly dividing his time and psyche between the two women – his impassioned wrangling with Dorothy is of course in marked contrast to the chaste, interrupted kiss he stole from Sandy in the diner. The sex session that follows extends the movie's notion of hyperbolised sexual experience – while Jeffrey is perfectly (and realistically) happy to rut with Dorothy in the traditional manner, his convenient division of fucking (Dorothy) from love (Sandy) collapses when Dorothy insists, 'I want you to hurt me.' In the film's purple take on things psychosexual, sex alone isn't trial enough for Jeffrey to pass from immaturity: he's got to experience the deviant nightmare of the primal scene he witnessed in order to 'gain experience'. What we're on to here is the idea of sex itself being essentially symbolic of a larger, more pervasive passage, mainly our necessary corruption and the loss of childhood ignorance, and since the film's universe is hyperbolised, so must be its carnal ordeal. 'I don't want to hurt you,' he whispers, 'I want to help you,' and tells her that he knows about her family's crisis. He never finishes – Dorothy loses control (as does the soundtrack, a rising wall of storm winds, gas hiss and edificial indigestion), begging to be hit so frantically that Jeffrey does, twice, hesitantly, but then with greater sureness. Lynch cuts to Dorothy's open, pleasured mouth, and dissolves to a torrent of flames.

There's no escaping that this moment is a sexual thrill for Jeffrey, Dorothy and Lynch alike (not to mention its reinforcement of Lynch's distant sympathy for Frank, by having Jeffrey identify with him in action), and the theorists could easily and correctly pigeonhole it as an instance of raw masculine wish-fulfilment, that Dorothy is 'inextricably implicated in sexual violence'.[31] Such ideological readings never quite wash with me, however, because they ignore vast amounts of imagery and information in efforts to hone in on often a single image and its

Mysteries of love: Jeffrey and Sandy

'signification', and because *Blue Velvet* in particular is so overt about its archetypes, and simultaneously so empathic with them, that it seems to have done a great deal of the interrogating on its own. Just look at how Lynch follows up that close-up: with a step-printed (slo-mo) shot of the two lovers in mid-coitus, accompanied by echoing, Splet-intensified animal noises on the soundtrack. To what degree are Lynch's masculine ideas about femininity and sex not confronted by the film itself? Where is the gap between the author and the text through which we can insinuate our prejudices?

'I still have you inside me,' Dorothy tells Jeffrey as he's leaving. 'It helps me.' To little or no extent does Jeffrey's deflowering provide him with power; this post-coital scene is stopped short by the entrance – with the heart-stopping shock of a voyeur suddenly locking eyes with the subject of his stare – of Frank stepping into the hallway, followed by his motley and buffoonish trio of henchmen (Brad Dourif, Jack Nance and J. Michael Hunter). Jeffrey may as well be ten years old here, answering Frank's taunts with frightened one-word replies, and being eventually grabbed by the collar of his jacket and shoved down the stairs. Frank begins to represent here a violent homosexual threat to Jeffrey; on their 'joyride', he's referred to as 'our pussy', and Jeffrey is subjected to a number of symbolic rapes. (The original script even has Dorothy threaten Jeffrey with the prospect of Frank 'opening' him.) This has been taken too literally by some as an incestuous twist on the oedipal theme; rather, it simply makes sense as a further purpling of sexual distress. The 'Dad' in Jeffrey's scenario is an abstracted agent of malice, and so his methods and behaviour, like that of a rapist of any stripe, are motivated more by hatred and rage than sexual longing. Of course, the father in a classic oedipal dynamic is only a haywire rapist in the eyes of the uncomprehending child, who mistakes sex for assault and sexual pleasure for pain.

Their first stop is Ben's (or, as the sign in the window says, This Is It, though some have allowed the dialogue in the car to entitle it Pussy Heaven, and the script refers to it as the Barbary Coast), and it is here that Lynch's free-associative conceptualising takes off into thoroughly original waters. What are we to make of Ben (Dean Stockwell)? There's certainly no established paradigm by which to measure him – the entire scene is a nether region of criminal sickness, conjured up by Lynch. Ben himself is apparently a drug dealer of some sort, a tanked-up, made-up, gameshow-host-outfitted, pansexual ghoul, sporting a cigarette holder with an unlit cigarette in it, an ear band, and the speech patterns of a Warhol Factory reject. Stockwell's performance here is unnerving – he seems to be utterly confident in the character's polymorphous perversity, but we still have no clue as to what exactly that perversity *is*. (The casting here is interesting: Stockwell is, with Hopper, a veteran of the psychedelic exploitation movies of the 60s, the first wave of anti-establishment, anti-family movies ever made in America; how does this collude with Lynch's conservative creation of a '50s–80s' timeframe? However Lynch intended it, it seems that perhaps he was unable also to find a role as well for Bruce Dern, and opted for his daughter instead.) Ben's place has its own seedy glow: cheap 50s-style furniture, tinny colours, a crew of badly wigged fat women in garish glasses sitting inexpressively around, waiting for orders. Lynch shot this scene as a series of stilted tableaux, with Frank's crew standing with Ben, Dorothy and Jeffrey in a flat mockery of cocktail party discomfort, interrupted only by Frank bellowing irrationally at his henchmen as if they're kids ('Let's have a beer with Ben!') and by the various teases and punches administered whimsically to Jeffrey. 'You are so fucking *suave*!' Frank proclaims several times, eliciting a fluttery smile from Ben. Here, Frank's 'fuck' quotient climbs with his state of tense inadequacy in front of Ben, whom he obviously admires; every other word is 'fuck', and often the word means nothing. 'Here's to your health, Frank,' purrs Ben, to which Frank says 'No, fuck, let's drink to something else. Let's drink to fucking!' 'Here's to your fuck,' Ben toasts gamely.

It's at Ben's, however, that Dorothy's family is being held hostage (the 'This Is It' sign therefore suggests that old Looney Tunes joke, wherein Daffy Duck or Bugs Bunny would find gangsters in a house

with a neon sign blinking 'Gangster's Hideout'). When Frank allows her
to visit them behind a closed door, Jeffrey listens intently to Dorothy's
wail: 'Donny! Donny! No! No! Donny, Mummy *loves* you!' We never
learn what happened to Dorothy's son while in captivity, but given the
company, and this outburst, it can't be pretty. To the side, Jeffrey
overhears Frank telling Ben about 'Gordon' taking 'all those drugs' away
(more fractured clues), and then conspiratorially muttering, 'The Candy
Coloured Clown They Call the Sandman', which Ben takes as a cue to
pick up a mechanic's trouble light and mouth into it as if it was a
microphone the words of Roy Orbison's 'In Dreams' (not in the original
script – was it improvised?). This tableau in particular is fraught with
desires and tensions the rest of the film only hints at: as Ben croons the
now-noxious Orbison ballad into the light, Frank stands a few paces

Ever been to Pussy Heaven? Ben (Dean Stockwell) air-croons Roy Orbison for Frank

away intently mouthing the words himself (who's imitating who?), at first with great earnestness and then with increasing agitation. The song *means* something to him, just as 'Blue Velvet' does, something soothing yet finally agonising. Or, perhaps, the pleasurable associations of the song fade too quickly. Ben, it seems, is performing *for* Frank, just as Dorothy performs, and with a similar clubfootedness. Everywhere Frank goes, someone is trying to appease him through ritualised psychodrama, and it always fails. He cannot sustain gratification – he is impotent, at odds not only with sexual pleasure, but with pleasure itself.

Ben sees Frank's implosion coming, stops singing and calmly strikes a pose, turning out the light. (You cannot see Stockwell do this on the video version; the whole scene is a triumph of startling wide-screen composition.) 'Now it's dark,' Frank says again, bidding a bashful

We're the same: Frank and Jeffrey face-off in the outlands

adieu to Ben and collecting his tribe. 'Let's FUCK!' he bellows in a forced attempt to regain his high spirits, 'I'll fuck anything that MOOOVES!' Lynch jump-cuts from his cackling mug to empty space and roaring car engines – the film can't keep up with him now.

In a distraught roadside break in the 'joyride', Frank gasses up, spitting 'Don't look at me, fuck!' at Jeffrey, allying him yet again in Frank's cosmos with Dorothy, as something to fuck, and then murmuring to Jeffrey as he fondles Dorothy in the front seat, 'You're like me.' Just as Jeffrey intuited so much about Dorothy's suicidal pathology, Frank intuits Jeffrey's role as a deviant; in fact, all of the film's characters seem to understand each other a great deal more than we understand them, which helps to give the film its seductive, hermetic allure. Frank and Jeffrey are not merely two sides of the same penny, or even neatly suppressed aspects of each other. Rather, Frank's impulses lurk in controllable form within Jeffrey, and Jeffrey's state of equilibrium is something Frank has lost. In the manner of Robin Wood's famous treatise on horror films, Frank could represent Jeffrey's (and our) 'surplus aggression', a cultural element exploding out of an environment dominated by social or sexual repression. Frank's condition, we're led to believe, is a product; indeed, come the film's mock-utopian ending, it's clear that Jeffrey's tribulation, from which he emerged whole, was one Frank had never sanely survived.

Jeffrey hollers, 'Hey, leave her alone!' Frank cannot believe his ears and, while looking at Jeffrey, pinches Dorothy's nipple hard enough to make her cry out. Jeffrey lashes out and punches him in the face, a singularly surprising act of machismo that incites the film's most searing violation of Jeffrey. Pulled from the car and held down by Frank's cronies, Jeffrey is kissed repeatedly by a lipstick-smeared Frank, who is muttering 'Pretty, pretty, pretty . . .', still another uneasy suggestion of parental violations in Frank's past. 'Paul!' Frank frantically issues a command to a henchman: 'Candy Coloured Clown!' When the Orbison song starts on the car stereo, a fat woman from Ben's who tagged along climbs up on to the car roof and starts to lethargically dance. 'I'll send you a love letter!' Frank howls into Jeffrey's smeared face, 'Straight from my heart, fucker! You know what a love letter is? A bullet from a fucking gun, fucker! You get a love letter from me, you're fucked forever!' And then, using his fingers as a second mouth, Frank recites the Orbison lyrics: In dreams, I walk with you / In dreams, I talk to you / In dreams, you're mine, all of the time, forever, in dreams.' He stuffs a shred of velvet into Jeffrey's mouth, makes him feel his muscles ('You like that?', another echo from Dorothy) and then beats the living daylights out of him.

The sequence is a heart-stopper of lunacy, absurdism and unreasonable visual pleasure, as Lynch cuts from Frank and Jeffrey, to Dorothy terrified in the car, to the woman dancing on the car, all set to the overripe, ridiculous pop song (which, even more than the titular song, can never be listened to calmly again). This scene manifests most clearly the role that pop songs play in Lynch's, and Frank's, cosmology: as sweet, innocuous tissues of lies. Like Lynch, whose adoration of pop music belies a cynical fascination with its daydreamy innocence, Frank is drawn to them even as they enrage him with their betrayals, their false sense of hope. It's obvious that the film's songs mean something radically different to Frank than they do to anyone else ('love letters' equals 'bullets' etc.). In any case, 'In Dreams' is apparently Frank's credo, at least as far as Jeffrey's concerned, in whose dreams Frank imagines he 'walks' etc. The homosexual subtext of this scene is barely 'sub', but it's all scrambled up with the various and conflicting oedipal hungers being played out; Frank can't make out if he's the Daddy, the Mommy or the Baby any more. He prepares for the beating in the same manner he prepared for sex; after all, the pleasure of it is not so fleeting, and commonly the last recourse to the otherwise impotent.

Jeffrey wakes up in the industrial wilds the next morning and makes his way home, where he suddenly bursts into tears amid flashbacks not only of his encounter with Frank but his abuse of Dorothy. At breakfast, Lynch lightens the mood considerably: Jeffrey's mother and aunt gasp at Jeffrey's bruises, prompting a 'I don't . . . want to talk about it.' You should talk about things, his aunt prattles, studies

show – and an exhausted but bemused Jeffrey cuts her off: 'Aunt
Barbara, I love you but you're gonna get it.'

Like a good Hardy Boy, Jeffrey knows when he's in over his head
and the authorities should take over, so he goes to Detective Williams's
house (after going to the station and glimpsing the Yellow Man, Frank's
'Gordon'), where Williams unblinkingly accepts his photographs and
story, but maintains a patriarchal sternness regarding Jeffrey's freelance
investigative work and Sandy's possible involvement.

After a high-school party (where the two dance to the lachrymose
Julee Cruise ballad 'Mysteries of Love'), Jeffrey and Sandy are driving
home when a car rearends them. 'It's Frank!' Jeffrey instinctively says as
he's being violated from behind. But no: 'It's Mike!' Sandy screams,
'Jeffrey, Oh my God!' Sandy thinks there's going to be real trouble now;
Jeffrey is visibly relieved – *thank God it's only a jealous football player*.
Mike (Ken Stovitz) is an unremarkable archetype of adolescent brawn
(except that he's blond, suggesting that Sandy's personal story is also
divided by light/dark dichotomies), beer-drunk and ready to kick ass.

In many interviews, Lynch has recounted a story from his
childhood wherein he and his little brother saw a naked woman walking
down the street one day, and his brother burst out crying at the sight.
It's a resonant image in how it reveals the power of inappropriate adult
behaviour on children; little Johnny Lynch knew such a sight violated his
limited knowledge of 'how things should be', and he knew the violation
was serious and meaningful, though we can assume he had little idea as
to why. Seeing through his brother's eyes in this story is, more or less,
Lynch's vision for the film in general: the inescapable yet tragic
confrontation of the innocent with the suffering and inequities of
adulthood. The scene derived from this memory is one of the few in the
film we can trace back to Lynch's past; again, who knows how many
other interfaces there are? Here, the pugnacious Mike squares off
against Jeffrey outside Jeffrey's house, and only the horrific sight of a
battered, naked Dorothy making her way zombie-like across the lawn
(all shot from a discreet, unmoving distance) prevents him. 'Who's that,

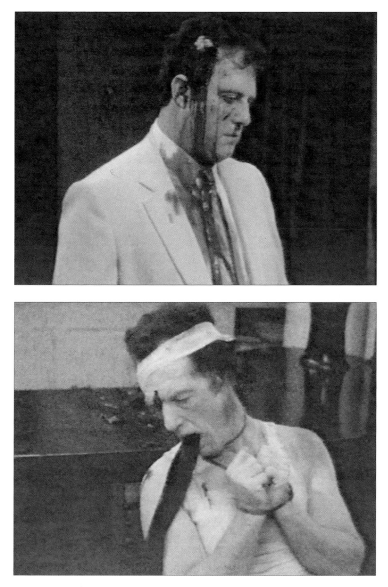

Don (Dick Green) and the Yellow Man (Fred Pickler) in Dorothy's kitchen: what happened?

your mother?' Mike instinctively taunts; it takes him a few moments to understand what he sees. When Jeffrey runs over to Dorothy and leads her back to the car, Mike becomes a befuddled apologist: 'I'm really . . . uh, I'm really sorry.' He even tries to grab Jeffrey, to make him understand, and Jeffrey squirms past him, allowing an 'It's okay'; MacLachlan's panicky handling of the scene adds the requisite Lynchian edge of ghastly humour to the whole situation.

Sandy is of course stunned by the complicit intimacy between Jeffrey and Dorothy, and Dern plays these difficult scenes with a breath-catching degree of honesty. Jeffrey drives to Sandy's house ('My father can get an ambulance quicker than anyone,' she says); Dern enters the house first in a dead fluster, calling out to her parents as if a nuclear warhead was coming through the front door and she just wants to let them know about it. Casting classic TV mom Hope Lange as Dern's mother was something of a viciously ironic stroke, as is evident here: Mrs Williams, in a plaid robe, answers her daughter's calls to find a bruised, raving naked woman in her living room. The film's evocation of parental fears is never so literal as it is in this scene. Here, the invasion of middle-class orthodoxy by sexual chaos is most graphically displayed; Lynch knows we're squirming, and so he just coolly lets us watch as Jeffrey tries to calm Dorothy down, and the Williamses look on in complete numb horror. It's here as well that Sandy must consider Jeffrey no longer as a boy but as a 'man' with a sexual life; Dorothy's standing unavoidably there twinned to him like the naked manifestation of his new sexual self, looming in the living room, a giant exposed erection, if you will. (Similar diagnoses could be made of Henry and his baby in *Eraserhead*, the giant worms in *Dune*, and Bobby Peru in *Wild at Heart*.) Such a reading is hardly reductive to Dorothy's character, since this would be only how she's viewed by Sandy, whose narrow window on the world is getting larger by the second. 'I love you!' Dorothy wails deliriously, 'Love me!' Sandy collapses with this declaration, followed up by Dorothy's gloating 'He put his disease in me!' This line is explained further in the original script, where Dorothy refers to Jeffrey's semen as men's 'disease', and their 'craziness'. (So much of the original script was cut, contributing to the film's suspended air, that Bret Wood, in *Video Watchdog*, termed Lynch's process 'creation by omission'.[32]) Eventually Mrs Williams covers her with a coat – a few moments too late, as far as we're concerned – and Dorothy begs Jeffrey to help Don, her husband. When the 50s-style ambulance comes and takes Dorothy away (she screams, significantly, 'I'm falling, I'm falling, help me!' after shaking off her oxygen mask), Sandy slaps Jeffrey hard, affronted by his betrayal not only in a literal you-cheated-and-lied sense, but also by voyaging into sexual territory without her – now, she's alone. Implicitly virginal, Sandy is left facing adulthood and the dark secrets of sex without a comrade. On the phone with Jeffrey (calling from the hospital), Sandy forgives him and then sobs 'Where is my dream?'

The film's climax is Jeffrey's return to the Deep River, where, in Dorothy's apartment, he finds the grisly vestiges of Frank Booth-style mayhem. This is Lynch's most inspired tableau, a vision of 50s, *LIFE* magazine-style kitchen convenience and Dantean grue: standing stock-still next to the kicked-in TV set (emitting a constant, Splet-devised buzz) is the Yellow Man, a head wound pouring blood and brain matter on to his signature jacket. That he's standing after such trauma is a neurological conundrum Lynch loves; in *Wild at Heart*, the protagonists happen upon a car accident from which Sherilyn Fenn stumbles, disassociated and searching for her purse even though her scalp is nearly falling off. The Yellow Man is still alive, barely: when the police radio in his pocket crackles, his arm involuntarily swings up and knocks the shade off a standing lamp (which, at scene's end, buzzes and burns out like the lights in *Eraserhead*). A few paces away from him sits Don, hogtied and gagged with velvet, his ear shorn off, a spray of blood and brain matter on the counter behind him. When Jeffrey first glimpses them, he quickly hides, but immediately realises they cannot see him. Watching them, an expression of sad exhaustion comes over Jeffrey: 'I'm going to let them find you on their own,' he tells the two bodies. Lynch brings up Ketty Lester's 'Love Letters' on the soundtrack (a chart-

(Overleaf) The director confronts the gunshot dummy of Dennis Hopper

topper in 1962), affords us a few glimpses of Detective Williams battling unseen suspects in a shoot-out, and has Jeffrey ruefully leave the apartment, shaking his head with sympathy and resignation.

But his combat with the father is far from over: seeing Frank approach downstairs (in the 'well-dressed man disguise' Jeffrey had photographed earlier), Jeffrey scrambles back to Dorothy's (Lynch can't resist a suspenseful key fumble at the door) and hides. He fishes the police radio out of the Yellow Man's pocket, contacts Detective Williams, and then (realising Frank can hear through *his* radio) decoys the telltale radio in the bedroom, dashing for his old sanctuary, the closet. Jeffrey's covert manoeuvrings have a charming Nancy Drew-like simplicity (as does Frank's 'disguise', which couldn't fool a blind man), but remain suspenseful, thanks to our harrowed knowledge of what's at stake. If Jeffrey's motivation for returning to Dorothy's is seriously unclear narratively speaking, Frank's is downright unfathomable; it's as if they're drones drawn back to the nest. (Anyway, to argue for completely sensible behaviour from these id-addled antagonists is to have not paid attention to the rest of the film.) 'You shit-for-brains, man, you forgot I have a police radio!' Frank hollers after kicking in the door, ripping off his disguise, taking his sweet time. 'One well-dressed fucking man knows where your fucking cute butt is hiding!' he continues, yanking the velvet swatch from Don's mouth, tying it to his gun and gassing up. We, like Jeffrey, see him from down the hall, preening a bit with the gas, the velvet tied around the gun's shaft like a ribbon on an erection. When he launches into the bedroom squealing 'Pretty, pretty!' and shoots the bed, Jeffrey sneaks out in a flash and grabs the Yellow Man's gun, readying himself with his own phallic weapon in the dark. (He could've run out the front door, but what closure would that provide, on any level?) Frank comes stalking him in full homicidal glory, searching the other rooms and, hilariously, clearing the decks of extraneous input: he first shoots the buzzing TV, silencing it, and then pumps another bullet into the Yellow Man, who finally, obediently, falls. Realising with a smile that Jeffrey's hiding in the closet, Frank preps with gas and slowly approaches the camera – we're seeing him head on, in sweaty close-up. Jeffrey steadies the gun, the door opens and he fires; the Splet-fashioned noise accompanying Frank's gunshot death sounds like an admixture of metallic skidding and animal shrieks. Sandy and Detective Williams appear in the door (Williams holds his gun and suspicious gaze on Jeffrey just a few moments too long), and Williams eventually says, 'It's all over, Jeffrey.'

And it is, too: Jeffrey's passage through his own oedipal torments has been completed, with the mother safe, the lost son returned and the father decimated for all time. Sandy and Jeffrey embrace in the hall, and Lynch whites out to a close-up of … Jeffrey's ear, the camera pulling back slowly, completing the cycle.

Is the idealised coda that follows a blind affirmation of authority and conformity, as disgruntled theorists have maintained? (That the film celebrates the banal over the deviant seems to upset many post-modern scholars.) It's hardly that 'normal', for one thing: set to the queerly ethereal 'Mysteries of Love', the scene has a drugged quality to it, from Jeffrey's sluggish movements getting up from his lawn chair, to Mr Beaumont's exaggerated gesture of reassurance ('Feeling much better now!') to the two Moms seated identically on the sofa, to that strange robin, which doesn't embody Sandy's dream so much as some creepy, dangerous, earthbound manifestation of it. Ready for lunch, Jeffrey, Sandy and Aunt Barbara watch the obviously mechanical bird sitting on the kitchen windowsill, a real live beetle gripped in its beak. 'It's a strange world, isn't it?' Sandy muses happily, and Lynch dissolves to the flower–fire-engine–flower triptych of the opening, and Dorothy playing with her blond-haired son in the grass, the first time in the entire film we see daylight touch her. A few strains of Dorothy's version of 'Blue Velvet' rise up, and Lynch pans to the cloudless sky. The ideal remains imbued with savagery; the formally traumatised and disordered universe between Jeffrey's ears is now superseded by the ambiguous, non-split outside world of the robin and the beetle, locked in predatory congress.

A strange world: Jeffrey and Sandy enjoy the recovered suburban paradise of Lynch's dreams, complete with a beetle-chewing clockwork robin

'That is the subject of *Blue Velvet*,' Lynch told a French interviewer. 'You apprehend things, and when you try to see what it's all about, you have to live with it.'[33] Hardly, as Karen Jaehne maintained in *Cineaste*, a close-minded warning 'against temptations to pursue knowledge'.[34] Questionable depictions of gender conflict notwithstanding, *Blue Velvet* is truer to Lynch's unironic, childlike view of life than post-modern theory permits, since it is remarkably free of judgments, and therefore of 'placements' of blame, culpability or oppressive intent. As a vision, the film accepts its conflicting components as they are, and though its lack of a convenient moral viewpoint has disturbed some, it has invigorated others. Indeed, the suspension of judgment is one of Jeffrey's graces, and perhaps what enabled him to weather the struggle to manhood in a strange world. The lack of same, it could be said, was Frank's ruination.

3

— **What were you thinking of, my child?**
— **I was thinking of heaven.**
    Lautréamont (trans. Paul Knight)

In a story recounted in *Movieline*, a friend of the magazine's editor
Virginia Campbell saw *Blue Velvet* in a New York theatre where a small
fire broke out in the middle of the movie. As smoke began to waft past
the screen image of Dennis Hopper kneeling between Isabella
Rossellini's legs whining 'Baby wants to *fuck*!' the theatre patrons
reluctantly, transfixedly, backed their way slowly up the aisles. When no
actual flames materialised, they slowly sat back down, their eyes never
leaving the screen. 'If you ask me,' Campbell wrote, 'that's
entertainment.'[35]

In the deepest meaning of the word, surely. *Blue Velvet* is one of
those cultural gifts that just keeps on giving. Its influences are
incalculable, and the laundry list of films bearing its teethmarks is long
and fascinating. Not only would *Wild at Heart*, *Twin Peaks* and *Fire Walk
with Me* have been impossible without its precedence; so would *Heart of
Midnight*, *Near Dark*, *Siesta*, *Heathers*, *Static*, *Dead Ringers*, *Zelly & Me*
(co-starring Lynch and Rossellini), Lewis Klahr's *Tales of the Forgotten
Future*, *Parents*, *Barton Fink*, *Hellraiser*, *Paperhouse*, *Apartment Zero*, *Santa
sangre*, *Sweetie*, *The Silence of the Lambs*, *The Reflecting Skin*, *Poison*,
Strange Days, *The Babysitter*, *Society*, *Seven*, *Reckless* and *Welcome to the
Dollhouse*, not to mention Lynch-offspring Jennifer's own, glibly
outrageous *Boxing Helena*. David Byrne's *True Stories*, Tim Hunter's
River's Edge, Jonathan Demme's *Something Wild* and Stuart Gordon's
From Beyond, all released the same year as *Blue Velvet*, inarguably share
its zeitgeist.

The bloodline runs directly to television and the post-*Velvet*
bizarrities of *Erie, Indiana*, *American Gothic*, *The X Files*, *Wild Palms*,
Lars von Trier's *The Kingdom* and *The Adventures of Pete and Pete*, the

first Lynchian children's show. Music videos, TV commercials and comics have co-opted the film's style and text; fiction by Katherine Dunn, Patrick McGrath, Thom Jones, Alice Hoffman, Tim Lucas, James Ellroy, Bret Easton Ellis and scores of lesser lights have used its basic materials; pop music by Nine Inch Nails, P.J. Harvey, Portishead, Jane's Addiction and Chris Isaak has borrowed its voice. The film may have even sparked off the renaissance in Roy Orbison's career before his death, as well as the brief but hallowed reuniting of the Velvet Underground. The resurgence of interest in artists like Robert Crumb (whose acclaimed biographical documentary *Crumb* Lynch executive produced), Jeff Wall, Joel-Pieter Witkin, Cindy Sherman, Joe Coleman, Edward Hopper, Joel Sternfeld and Diane Arbus could be read as *Blue Velvet* aftershock, as could the entire culture's still-accelerating embrace

Frightful knowledge: *The X Files*

of things deviant and 'weird': suddenly, in the mid-80s, the middle of the Reagan era, sadomasochism and permanent body art became fashionable, suburban sex crimes were unavoidable headline news, drag queens became media personalities, and every form of mundane domestic violence and lower-middle-class derangement became fodder for daytime TV, and on a truly Brobdingnagian scale. With his little parable of sexual awakening and fear, Lynch mainlined deviancy and psychosexual angst right into the cultural mainstream. With just a few years left before the millennium, we're still watching the waters rise.

But it's just a movie, right? Perhaps the grandest wonder about *Blue Velvet* is how it retains its mystery and power and resists being reduced by familiarity or analysis of any variety or quantity, something to which only a handful of films can lay claim. In international film culture

(Left) Now it's dark: Hopper as the unforgettable Frank. (Above) Rossellini in repose

(especially in America and France), seeing the film has become something of a rite all its own, a gauntlet anyone serious about cinema must run. Lynch's subsequent career has indeed suffered its fair share of misfires and peccadilloes, and it may be, as several critics have suggested, that *Blue Velvet* will be Lynch's *Citizen Kane*, that he'll never approach its achievement again. No one should be surprised if this turns out to be the case. *Blue Velvet* is a vision of life seen through eyes bloodshot with desire. There's something elusively seductive about it, as if its colour schemes, pregnant rhythms and hellzapoppin imagery were designed to mask a subliminal traction, pulling us in without our conscious consent. It may simply be that *Blue Velvet* has captured the ambience of subconscious human wildlife more vividly than any film before or since.

Notes

1 J. Hoberman, 'Return to Normalcy', *The Village Voice*, 22 September 1986.

2 Virginia Campbell, 'Something Really Wild', *Movieline*, September 1990.

3 'If you could put into words the symbolic equivalent to most of my visual concepts, no one would probably want to produce my films. I don't know what a lot of things mean. I just have the feeling that they are right or not right. . . . My first inspiration is life, therefore everything makes sense because it is linked to life.' Lynch interviewed in *Cineaste* vol. 15 no. 3, 1987.

4 The film was only nominated for one Academy Award, Best Director, the only nomination courtesy of the Directors Guild of America; that the AMPAS acknowledged such a controversial film at all is a miracle. Dennis Hopper was also nominated, as Best Supporting Actor for *Hoosiers*, which, it is commonly held, was their waffling way of commending his extraordinary work in Lynch's film.

5 Hoberman, 'Return to Normalcy'.

6 Pauline Kael, 'Out There and In Here', *The New Yorker*, 22 September 1986.

7 Roger Ebert, *Chicago Sun-Times*, 19 September 1986.

8 Pat H. Broeske, 'Outtakes', *Los Angeles Times*, 28 September 1986.

9 Anne Thompson, 'Risky Business', *L.A. Weekly*, 3 October, 1986.

10 Barry Gifford, *The Devil Thumbs a Ride & Other Unforgettable Films* (New York: Grove, 1988), pp. 21–2.

11 Ralph Rugoff, 'Wild at Heart' *Premiere* vol. 4 no. 1, September 1990.

12 Ed Naha, *The Making of 'Dune'* (London: W.H. Allen, 1984).

13 In conversation with the author, November 1995.

14 Lynch interviewed in *Le Cinéphage* no. 6, May–June 1992.

15 Rugoff, 'Wild at Heart'.

16 *Positif* no. 356, October 1990.

17 *Box Office*, April 1981.

18 James Greenberg, '"Blue Velvet" Next Film for "Dune's" Lynch', *Variety*, 31 August, 1984.

19 Brett Wood, 'Bluer Velvet', *Video Watchdog* vol. 4, March/April 1991. All of my quotes from the original screenplay were first quoted in this generally fastidious and invaluable magazine.

20 'It had to be an ear because it's an opening. An ear is wide and you can go down into it. It goes somewhere vast.' Lynch interviewed in *Cineaste*.

21 There's a significance for Lynch, who in taking his name off the re-edited TV version of *Dune*, replaced his directing credit with the Directors Guild standard pseudonym 'Allen Smithee', and his writing credit with 'Judas Booth'.

22 Michel Chion, *David Lynch* (London: BFI Publishing, 1995), p. 12.

23 Kael, 'Out There and In Here'.

24 'Take One', *People*, 20 October 1986.

25 Lynne Layton, '*Blue Velvet*: A Parable of Male Development', *Screen* vol. 35 no. 4, Winter 1994.

26 Wood, 'Blue Velvet'.

27 Layton, '*Blue Velvet*: A parable of Male Development'.

28 Chion, *David Lynch*, pp. 93–7.

29 Jane M. Shattuc, 'Postmodern Misogyny in *Blue Velvet*', *Genders* no. 13, Spring 1992.

30 Karen Jaehne, 'Blue Velvet', *Cineaste* vol. 15 no. 3, 1987.

31 Wood, 'Blue Velvet'.

32 Lynch interviewed in *La Revue du cinéma* no. 403, February 1987.

33 Jaehne, 'Blue Velvet'.

34 Campbell, 'Something Really Wild'.

Credits

USA

1986

Production company

Dino De Laurentiis
Entertainment Group Inc.
A David Lynch Film

Executive producer

Richard Roth

Producer

Fred Caruso

Production supervisor

Gail M. Kearns

Production manager

Fred Caruso

**Production office
co-ordinator**

Kathryn Colbert

Location co-ordinator

Morris Atkins

Locations assistant

Edward Brown

Key production assistant

John Wildermuth

Production assistants

Jennifer Lynch, Robert Kearns,
Patti Clark, Steve Day, Roe
Fonvielle, Celia Claire Barnes

Auditor

Rita M. Lucibello

Assistant accountants

Cindy Jo Gray, Kathi Levine

Production secretary

Sarah Christine Davis

Assistant to David Lynch

John Wentworth

Intern associates

Peter Braatz, Frank Behnke

Director

David Lynch

First assistant director

Ellen Rauch

Second assistant director

Ian Woolf

Script supervisor

Rina Sternfeld

Casting

Johanna Ray, Pat Golden

Casting associate

Pam Rack

Extras/additional casting

Mark Fincannon and
Associates

Screenplay

David Lynch

Director of photography

Frederick Elmes

First assistant camera

Lex Dupont

Camera assistant

David Rudd

Key grip

Donne Daniels

Dolly grip

Mark Davis

Grip department

Tony Stephens,
Jeff Williams

Best boy

Joe Maxwell

Gaffer

Michael Katz

Electric department

Dave Salamone, Denis
Shelton, Neil Holcomb,
Roger Russ, Monte Dhoge,
Tim Farrow

Rigging chief

Steve Venetis

Rigging department

James Tamaro, Doug Hersh,
Austin Gross,
Mike Hall, Jay Yawler,
Ross Kolman, David Strong,
Jock Brandis, Robert Hoelen

Stills photographer

Umberto Montiroli

Music/music conductor

Angelo Badalamenti

Music performed by

Film Symphony of Prague

Music editor

Mark Adler

Assistant music editor

Sandina Bailo-Lape

Music re-recording mixer

Todd Boekelheide

Songs

'Blue Velvet' by Lee Morris,
Bernie Wayne, performed by
Bobby Vinton, Isabella
Rossellini; 'Blue Star' by
Angelo Badalamenti, David
Lynch, performed by Isabella
Rossellini; 'Love Letters' by
Victor Young, Edward
Heyman, performed by Ketty
Lester; 'Mysteries of Love' by
Angelo Badalamenti, David
Lynch, performed by Julee
Cruise; 'In Dreams'
by/performed by Roy
Orbison; 'Honky Tonk
(Part I)' by Shep Shepherd,
Clifford Scott, Bill Doggett,
Billy Butler, performed by Bill
Doggett; 'Livin' for Your
Lover', 'Gone Ridin'
performed by Chris Isaak

Editor

Duwayne Dunham

Assistant editors

Jonathan Shaw,
Mary Sweeney

Apprentice editors

Brian Berdan, Tim Craig

Special effects

Greg Hull, George Hill

Production designer

Patricia Norris

Chief scenic artist
Robert Testerman
Scenic artist
Tanya Lowe
Props/set dressing
Michael Anderson, Vernon
Harrell, Loren McNamara,
Paul Sebastian, Arron Waitz,
Doug White
Draftsperson
Dawn Serody
Construction
co-ordinator
Les Pendleton
Art department assistant
Catherine Davis
Lead carpenter
Tim Viereck
Prop master
Tantar Leviseur
Set prop man
Shawn Burney
Set wardrobe
Henry Earl Lewis
Costume shop supervisor
Gloria Laughride
Hair stylist
Barbara Page
Make-up supervisor
Jeff Goodwin
Special effects make-up
Dean Jones
Titles/opticals
Van Der Veer Photo Effects
Sound design
Alan Splet
Sound mixer
Ann Kroeber
Sound editors
Bob Fruchtman,
Pat Jackson
Dialogue editors
Vivien Gilliam, John Nutt,
Michael Silvers
Assistant sound editors
Karen Brocco, John Berbeck,

John Norris, Sarah
Rothenberg, Page Sartorius,
Alan Abrams
Sound effects editor
Richard Hyams
Re-recording mixers
Mark Berger, David Parker
Sound assistant
Frank Eulner
Boom operator
Patrick Moriarty
Foley artist
Dennie Thorpe
Negative cutter
Donnah Bassett
Generator operator
Frank Williams
Craft service
Mary Bridges
Transportation
co-ordinator
Patricia Hill
Drivers
Welch Lambeth, John
Bankson, Doug Du Rose,
Cynthia Jarose
Stunt co-ordinator
Richard Langdon
Stunt performers
David Boushey, Reginald
Barnes Jr., W. Mark
Fincannon, Sherri Ann
Langdon, John W. McEuen,
Robert Burton, Dean
Mumford, Debra
Schuckman, Ken Sprunt Jr.
Isabella Rossellini
Dorothy Vallens
Kyle MacLachlan
Jeffrey Beaumont
Dennis Hopper
Frank Booth
Laura Dern
Sandy Williams
Hope Lange
Mrs Williams

Dean Stockwell
Ben
George Dickerson
Detective Williams
Priscilla Pointer
Mrs Beaumont
Frances Bay
Aunt Barbara
Jack Harvey
Tom Beaumont
Ken Stovitz
Mike
Brad Dourif
Raymond
Jack Nance
Paul
J. Michael Hunter
Hunter
Dick Green
Don Vallens
Fred Pickler
Yellow Man
Philip Markert
Dr Gynde
Leonard Watkins
Moses Gibson
Double Ed
Selden Smith
nurse Cindy
Peter Carew
coroner
Jon Jon Snipes
Little Donny
Andy Badale
piano player
Jean-Pierre Viale
Master of Ceremonies
Donald Moore
desk sergeant
A. Michelle Depland
Michelle Sasser
Katie Reid
party girls
Sparky
the dog

Bibliography

Broeske, Pat H. 'Outtakes',
Los Angeles Times,
28 September 1986.

Campbell, Virginia,
'Something Really Wild',
Movieline, September 1990.

Chion, Michel, *David Lynch*
(London: BFI Publishing,
1995).

Cineaste vol. 15 no. 3
(1987). This issue features
Laurent Bouzereau's
interview with Lynch, as well
as one of the most notoriously
blinkered of *Blue Velvet*
reviews, by Karen Jaehne.

Le Cinéphage no. 6,
May/June 1992. This issue
includes a dossier on Lynch
compiled by Paul Grave.

Gifford, Barry, *The Devil
Thumbs a Ride & Other
Unforgettable Films*
(New York: Grove, 1988).

Hoberman, J., 'Return to
Normalcy', *The Village Voice*,
22 September 1986.

Kael, Pauline, 'Out There
and In Here', *The New
Yorker*, 22 September 1986.

Kaleta, Kenneth C.,
David Lynch (New York:
Twayne, 1993).

Layton, Lynne, '*Blue Velvet*:
A Parable of Male
Development', *Screen*
vol. 35 no. 4, Winter 1994.

Naha, Ed, *The Making of
'Dune'* (London:
W.H. Allen, 1984).

Pellow, Kenneth C., '*Blue
Velvet* Once More', *Literature
Film Quarterly* vol. 18 no. 3,
1990. This is a special issue
of *LFQ* centring on the film;
several other articles are of
interest.

Positif no. 356, October
1990. This issue features an
interview with Lynch by
Michel Ciment and Hubert
Niogret as well as other
articles on Lynch.

La Revue du cinéma
no. 403, February 1987. This
issue includes Marie-Jose
Simpson's interview with
Lynch.

Rugoff, Ralph, 'Wild at
Heart', *Premiere* vol. 4 no. 1,
September 1990.

Shattuc, Jane M.,
'Postmodern Misogyny in
Blue Velvet', *Genders*,
no. 13, Spring 1992.

Stern, Lesley, 'The Oblivious
Transfer: Analyzing *Blue
Velvet*', *Camera Obscura* no.
30, May 1992.

Thomson, David,
*A Biographical Dictionary of
Film* 3rd edn. (New York:
Knopf, 1994).

Thompson, Anne, 'Risky
Business', *L.A. Weekly*,
3 October 1986.

Wallace, David Foster,
'David Lynch Keeps His
Head', *Premiere* vol. 10
no. 1, September 1996.

Wood, Bret, 'Bluer Velvet',
Video Watchdog vol. 4,
March/April 1991.

BFI Modern Classics is an exciting new series which combines careful research with high quality writing about contemporary cinema. Authors write on a film of their choice, making the case for its elevation to the status of classic. The series will grow into an influential and authoritative commentary on all that is best in the cinema of our time.

If you would like to receive further information about future **BFI Modern Classics** or about other books on film, media and popular culture from BFI Publishing, please fill in your name and address and return this card to the BFI*.

No stamp needed if posted in the UK, Channel Islands, or Isle of Man.

NAME

_____

ADDRESS

_____

POSTCODE

_____

* North America: Please return your card to:
Indiana University Press, Attn: LPB, 601 N Morton Street,
Bloomington, IN 47401-3797

BFI Publishing
21 Stephen Street
FREEPOST 7
LONDON W1E 4AN